Wills Guide
for America

Robert C. Waters

Self-Counsel Press Inc.
(a subsidiary of)
International Self-Counsel Press Ltd.

Canadian Cataloguing in Publication Data

Waters, Robert C.
   Wills Guide for America

(Self-counsel legal series)
ISBN 1-55180-283-X

   1. Wills—United States—Popular works.   2. Estate planning—United States—
Popular works. I. Title. II. Series

   KF755.W37 2001   346.7305'2   C2001-910318-2

Self-Counsel Press Inc.
(a subsidiary of)
International Self-Counsel Press Ltd.

1704 N. State Street
Bellingham, WA 98225
USA

1481 Charlotte Road
North Vancouver, BC V7J lHl
Canada

Contents

Introduction

For most people, part of the purpose of everyday life is providing for themselves and their loved ones and planning for the future. But few people realize estate planning — preparing for what happens after you die — has exactly the same purpose. In estate planning, perhaps the single most important action a person can take is to prepare a well-written will.

Writing a will is often really a simple matter. A husband may just want to leave everything to his wife, or vice versa. Or parents may seek to divide their assets equally among their children. This book is for people like these. It explains in everyday language how you can create and update your own will.

This book can also help you identify any problems that would require you to seek professional advice, and can help you understand how to discuss these problems in an informed manner with a professional. One key purpose of this book is *not* to raise unrealistic expectations about what you can do on your own. In the long run, professional advice is often far less costly than correcting a mistake you made on your own, especially if that mistake affects your loved ones after you are gone.

Part 1 of this book, Chapters 1 through 6, reviews the basics of estate planning and the considerations of preparing a well-written will. You should read this section before you begin to write your own will. It will give you a better understanding of the issues that may arise as you make your plans and talk to professionals. Then, once you complete your estate inventory, as shown in Sample 1, you will be well organized and prepared to establish a solid estate plan and write an effective will that reflects your wishes.

Part 2 of the book, Chapter 7, gets down to the nitty gritty. It takes you through the requirements of preparing a will and shows samples of various clauses that you may consider including when writing your own will.

Finally, Part 3, Chapter 8, covers the special topic of living wills (also known as advance directives) and powers of attorney. This is an issue that you would probably rather avoid, because it means thinking about a time in your life when you may be unable to control your own affairs. But dealing with the future, for better or worse, is essential in completing the task of estate planning. Preparing a living will and a power of attorney will give you the peace of mind that comes with knowing you have taken all the steps possible to make life easier for your loved ones. That is the ultimate goal of estate planning.

Part 1

**Wills and Estate Planning:
An Introduction**

1. The Importance of Estate Planning

1. Do You Need a Will?

Many people do not realize that if they die without a will, their property will be distributed to survivors according to formulas set by state laws. These laws say who *must* receive the property of any person who dies without a will. Every state has laws of this type, though the formulas they use vary. In many cases, these formulas will not reflect your true wishes regarding who should get your property after you die. Let's consider two examples:

> **EXAMPLE:** David and his wife Suzanne had three grown children, one of whom was developmentally disabled and entirely dependent on his parents. The other two were grown and self-sufficient. The bulk of the family's assets were in David's name, and he always intended that all of his property should go to his wife on his death to help care for the dependent child. But David died without signing a will. Under the law of his state, all of his property was divided into shares, with his wife and each child receiving a share. The result was that Suzanne had to care for the dependent child with only a portion of her husband's property, not the full estate.

EXAMPLE: Adrienne never married or had children. When she grew old, she developed a special bond with a young married couple who lived nearby. They cared for Adrienne through several illnesses. Though the couple contacted Adrienne's relatives, none ever came to visit her. As a result, Adrienne often said she wanted to leave everything she owned to this young couple, who were struggling to rear two children on the husband's meager salary. But Adrienne died suddenly without leaving a will. Under the law of her state, all of her property went to a distant cousin Adrienne had not seen in more than 50 years. The neighbor couple received nothing.

Court records are full of stories of people like these, who simply did not realize what would happen if they left no will. The only way to avoid this kind of scenario is to make sure you have a valid will. In plain terms, *if you do not decide who gets your property, the state decides for you.*

If you are fortunate enough to have a large estate, it is essential to have not only a will, but also a complete estate plan, and you may wish to enlist the help of professionals. There are two reasons for this. First, federal or state estate taxes could take a large piece of your estate after your death. With careful planning, you can reduce these taxes. The ways of doing so, however, are complex, and you should enlist the help of professionals such as estate or tax lawyers or accountants.

Second, lawyers and other professionals can use special legal tools to make sure your loved ones receive your property with a minimum of delay. There also are legal ways to have your assets professionally managed on behalf of loved ones who may be unable to manage these assets on their own. To take advantage of these special legal tools, you will need the help of a lawyer skilled in estate planning. The cost of the fee is well worth the trouble and expense your loved ones might endure without proper planning.

2. What Is Estate Planning?

Estate planning is a legal term used to describe the management of your affairs to reach your goal of providing, in future, for yourself and others, and it includes more than just deciding who will receive your money and property when you die. Estate planning also includes many things that must be done while you are still alive: any day-to-day decisions you make that affect how much property you own, how much money you accumulate, how much tax you must pay, and how many debts you owe. Estate planning, in other words, is not a one-time or occasional concern, but is an issue you confront every day. Most important, when you are planning your estate, your focus cannot be only on what happens after your death, but must also be on what happens during the remainder of your life. Understanding this concept will help you avoid the five biggest mistakes you can make in estate planning:

(a) Failure to update your will when necessary

(b) Failure to avoid problems or mistakes that will delay settling your estate after your death

(c) Failure to leave your loved ones the greatest possible amount of money or property under the law

(d) Failure to provide yourself with a comfortable life and retirement while still providing for your loved ones

(e) Failure to get the advice of professionals

2.1 Updating your will

You must update your will regularly to reflect the changing circumstances of your life. Marriage, divorce, the birth of children, or the deaths of loved ones are all reasons to update your will. Under many state laws, for example, a will that fails to provide adequately for spouses or children — especially minor children — sometimes must be modified *by law* to include them. There can be other complications, too, if your will is not updated. For instance, if all the people named in your will have died, your estate could go to relatives who you really do not want to receive it.

Writing a will, in other words, is not a one-time event in your life. You should review your will at least yearly to make sure it is still up-to-date, and again whenever your circumstances change significantly.

2.2 Avoiding delays in settling your estate

Poor planning can also lead to delays in settling your estate. Failure to update your will and mistakes in drafting it are perhaps the most serious problems, since they can lead to disputes or even lawsuits. At the very least, a delay could force your loved ones to live in reduced circumstances while they await the final settlement of your estate. At worst, delays could result in huge expenses that could have been avoided.

There are notorious cases in which attorneys' fees and other expenses have eaten up all or most of an estate before it could be settled. If your goal is to provide for loved ones, it makes no sense to let poor planning divert your money and property to people other than those you love.

> **EXAMPLE:** Oscar signed a will shortly after his marriage to Kate and before any children were born. Its main clause said simply, "I give everything I own to my dear wife, Kate." He never thought about the matter again. Years went by. Oscar and Kate had three children but divorced shortly after their tenth wedding anniversary. Oscar went on to remarry and had two more children before he died of a sudden heart attack. The settling of his estate, however, was delayed by a lawsuit involving his first and second wives and the children of both marriages. It wasn't until two years after his death that the estate was finally settled. Attorneys' fees and costs reduced Oscar's estate to a fraction of its original worth that meant little when divided among all his heirs.

Other things can cause delays, too. One common mistake is the failure to gather important documents about your property in one place where they will be safe yet easily accessed. You should make sure that those who will be involved in settling your estate know how to find these documents. It also is very helpful for you to write out a complete inventory of everything you own and include it with your estate documents. (See Chapter 6 for more information on preparing an inventory of your estate.)

2.3 Providing for loved ones

People most often write wills to provide for their loved ones. In many instances, their loved ones are people thought to be their "natural heirs," such as a spouse, children, or other blood relatives. However, some people also want to leave some of their assets to persons or organizations that would not be considered natural heirs. If, for example, you want to leave $10,000 of your estate to the Humane Society, you must have a will that says so *unless* you intend to give the money during your lifetime.

There also are a growing number of households consisting of couples who, though they are life partners, are not married to each other. A will is absolutely vital if you wish to leave some or all of your assets to an unmarried partner. Failure to have a valid will could result not only in that life partner receiving nothing, but perhaps also being forced out of the home you shared with him or her if it wasn't owned jointly. (**Note:** The State of Vermont may be an exception to this rule under recent legislation extending to life partners many of the same rights enjoyed by married couples. However, it is still a wise precaution to have your intentions plainly stated in a will, to leave no doubt.)

There is another factor to consider in providing for loved ones. Wills, though very important, are not always the total solution to estate planning. There are other methods of transferring property or money that can be vital in planning your estate and that can help ensure that you leave the maximum amount of money or property to your loved ones. These include special ways of transferring property while you are still alive and special ways of transferring property upon your death so that it automatically goes to the people for whom you want to provide. These alternative methods are crucial because they can, for example, reduce estate taxes or place money or property beyond the reach of your creditors after your death. That is why good estate planning is as important for the rich as it is for those whose debts may exceed the total value of their money or property — and for everyone in between. If your goal is to leave your loved ones as well off as possible, good planning is *always* required. As a rule, you should always seek professional advice if you think these alternative methods of transferring property might be helpful to you and those you love. (See Chapters 3 and 4 for a more detailed discussion of estate planning options.)

2.4 Providing for yourself

There is yet another aspect of estate planning all too commonly overlooked, and that is managing your money and property during your lifetime to create a comfortable life and retirement for yourself while also providing for those you love after your death. When you provide for yourself, you also tend to do a better job of providing for others. This does not necessarily mean hoarding money or foregoing luxuries, but it does mean taking prudent steps to protect assets that you really do not intend to spend or lose.

One of the most important planning tools is insurance. If you are not properly insured for illness, disability, and other risks of life, your estate could be reduced to nothing in short order, leaving nothing for your retirement and nothing for your heirs. That is why it is common for people to obtain not only health and disability insurance, but also supplemental forms of insurance to cover particularly expensive illnesses or injuries. Examples are excess major medical insurance, cancer insurance, intensive care insurance, and long-term care (nursing home) insurance.

Life insurance is yet another way of leaving something more for your heirs. In many instances, your employer's personnel office can help you understand the kinds of insurance that are available and the risks they cover. You also need to seek legal and tax advice if the proceeds of your insurance policies would make your estate taxable, since there are ways to reduce these taxes. (See Chapter 4.) Always keep in mind that life insurance paid to your loved ones is usually considered a part of your estate and can be subject to federal or state estate taxes.

Another important health-related issue is what you want others to do if you become so ill that your life can be sustained only by artificial means. "Advance directives" (often called "living wills") allow you to put in writing whether or not you want your life to be artificially prolonged. The decision to sign — or not to sign — an advance directive can have a significant impact on your estate, too. Artificial life support can be very expensive, and if you are not covered by insurance, could greatly reduce the value of your estate — something that is a pointless waste if it is not what you really want. (See Chapter 8 for a detailed discussion of living wills.)

Yet another important estate-planning tool is a basic understanding of the different ways of owning property or holding money. Your knowledge in this area can make or break your plans for a good income and retirement — and your plans for providing for loved ones. For instance, the US tax code allows for methods of holding financial assets so that they are not taxed for many years, allowing them to grow into staggering sums of money if properly invested. These include "deferred compensation" tools such as the popular 401(k) accounts available through many employers and Individual Retirement Accounts (IRAs) available through banks and other financial institutions. Planning is essential to make these tools work for you, since your individual circumstances might favor some methods over others. And, fortunately, advice on such investments often can be obtained for little or no cost from your employer's personnel office or from your financial institution.

Likewise, you need to understand the ways in which you currently own real estate, bank accounts, and other forms of property. Sometimes you can change to other forms of ownership that will better suit your long-term goals, though you should seek professional advice in doing so. Failure to understand the ways you currently own your property can lead to serious mistakes during estate planning. Some changes in methods of ownership also can have tax consequences for you and your loved ones.

2.5 Getting advice from professionals

Finally, signing a will is only one step in a process that starts with an analysis of your income, property, and debts, along with designing a strategy to reach your estate-planning goals. Truly good estate planning also includes assistance from different professional advisers such as your employer's personnel officer, a lawyer, a banker, an accountant, a trust officer, an insurance agent, and/or an investment or financial adviser.

Keep in mind that while some professionals charge a fee for their advice, others do not. For example, your employer's personnel officer may well be one of the most important professionals in helping you deal with questions about your insurance and deferred compensation. And this advice is almost always free. Take advantage of it.

2 Getting Started: The First Steps toward Successful Estate Planning

1. The Basics of Estate Planning

Just as there are five major mistakes often made in estate planning (see Chapter 1), there also are five major steps to helping you avoid those mistakes:

(a) Understanding what you own and how you own it

(b) Deciding who will get your money and property

(c) Setting goals for your estate

(d) Implementing your goals

(e) Reviewing your plans regularly

These five steps will help you determine your current state of affairs, the changes you want to make, and what you must do to make those changes.

1.1 Understanding what you own and how you own it

The first step is to inventory all your property and debts. Include anything of value, and be careful not to overlook things like insurance policies, deferred compensation accounts, or retirement benefits that could be payable to others after your death. You should try to value each item at current fair market value with an eye toward future increases in value. Doing so will help you estimate your taxes and income under various conditions. You should also examine and assemble documents concerning property ownership, including deeds, mortgages, and automobile titles. Do not overlook your existing will if you have one.

Make special note of any information contained in these documents that shows exactly *how* you own property. Do other people's names appear on these documents? For example, do bank accounts include special notations such as POD (payable on death), followed by a person's name? Do property deeds show that you jointly own real estate with another person "with right of survivorship"? Don't worry if you don't understand these terms now; they are explained elsewhere in this book. The important thing to remember at this stage is that you need to find out if there are any special terms of ownership on your property so that you can plan ahead. Chapter 6 provides more detail on how to go about preparing an inventory of your estate.

1.2 Deciding who gets your property

The second step is to analyze your present state of affairs to see who your beneficiaries — those who will receive your property or money when you die — are. If you already have a will, check to see what property will pass under it, what will not, and who gets what. Check your insurance policies, retirement accounts, or deferred compensation accounts to see if any beneficiaries are named in them. Examine your deeds to property and automobile titles. Note any problems. (For example, if one of these documents lists as joint owner someone who has died, you will need to change it.) The same may be true of documents that give property rights to someone you have divorced or someone you no longer want to be your beneficiary. Make note if it appears that your debts exceed your assets.

Once you know exactly what you own and who your named beneficiaries are, you can consider any changes you might want to make and decide who you want to receive your remaining property and money after your death. As you complete this process, be sure to gather all important documents about your property in a safe place, and include a full inventory of everything you own, where it is located, and how to obtain more information about it. (**Note:** You should read further in this book before you complete this step.)

1.3 Setting goals for your estate

Once you are sure that you know what you own and who you want your property to go to following your death, the next step is to set your goals for the years ahead. To make certain that you are getting maximum return on your investments at minimum tax cost, you may wish to seek the advice of professionals. For instance, talk to your employer's personnel office to see if there are ways you can reduce your income taxes while putting money aside for retirement, such as deferred compensation accounts. Under federally approved deferred compensation programs, you not only delay paying any income taxes on income you put into these accounts, but you also pay no income taxes on the interest you earn until you begin taking money back out of the account. Some people have actually turned deferred compensation accounts into a major source of wealth by investing wisely.

If your estate is likely to be substantial when you die, consult with lawyers, accountants, or other professionals who can help you plan more effectively and minimize any state or federal estate taxes you may owe. You also should consult professionals if there is a chance someone will challenge your will. For example, this might happen if you want to disinherit anyone who would be considered a natural heir, such as a daughter or son. You also want to be sure you have provided for sufficient cash funds to meet expenses at your death so that your property does not have to be sold at distress prices. Most important, you want to make sure that your property will go to the beneficiaries for whom you intend it.

1.4 Implementing your goals

Preparing your will is key to successfully implementing your estate-planning goals. If you do not have a will, you will need one, and if you already have a will, you should review it. No estate plan is complete without a valid will. But you also may decide to change one or more of your investments, restructure ownership of certain assets, sign a trust agreement, buy more insurance, or establish or update a deferred compensation account or IRA. You might want to change beneficiaries, sign a living will, or make some lifetime gifts. These estate-planning techniques are discussed more fully later in this book.

1.5 Reviewing your plans regularly

It is a good idea to periodically review your financial inventory and all your documents to make certain that they still reflect your goals. Doing so is just as important as having a regular physical examination by your doctor. For instance, you can conduct your review of your estate when you are gathering documents to prepare federal income taxes each year, since those papers will indicate the ways your property and income are changing. If an accountant is preparing your tax return, you may want to ask him or her for additional advice on how any changes in your circumstances affect your estate-planning goals. A sudden inheritance or an unexpected debt can dramatically alter the strategy you will need to take in planning for the future.

Whatever else you do, never fail to review and update your plans regularly. At a minimum, you should make sure documents about your property are easy to find and that you write out or update an inventory of your property to reflect any changes. Include the location of each item of property and where records about the property are located or the name and contact information of anyone who is the keeper (often called a custodian) of these records. Also keep in mind that you need to update your will as soon as possible after significant changes in your life such as the following:

- Marriage, remarriage, or divorce
- The birth of children, whether born in a marriage or not
- The adoption of children
- The birth of grandchildren
- The death of parents, a spouse, or a child
- The death of anyone named in your will
- Your decision to remove someone from your will
- Your decision to disinherit a family member
- A windfall such as an inheritance
- Your debts becoming unmanageable
- Your property growing enough to be taxed on your death
- Your moving to another state
- Your obtaining property in more than one state

Finally, a substantial number of decisions made in estate planning can affect taxes that you, your estate, or your survivors may owe. Tax problems are so common in estate planning that many lawyers who work in the field also have specialized training in tax law or rely on accountants to help them. It is always wise to consult in advance with a licensed accountant in your state to make sure you are not creating needless tax problems for yourself or your loved ones.

2. Understanding the Language of Wills and Estate Planning

Special words are used by lawyers and judges to describe the estate-planning process and the way it is supervised by judges. To get the most from this book and to see how estate planning works, you need to understand the basic terms and concepts. (Some of the more complex terms are discussed later in this book as they arise.)

2.1 What is a will?

A *will* is a legal document signed by you in the presence of witnesses. It declares how you want your property to be distributed after your death. A will has no legal effect until its validity has been proven through a process called *probate*. Most important, a will deals only with a specific kind of property called your *probate property*. (See Chapter 3 for a discussion of the difference between probate property and nonprobate property.)

Any addition to a will made after it has been signed is called a *codicil*. It is usually better to simply revise an entire will rather than to try to modify it with a codicil. Revising the document helps avoid the confusion and problems that can occur if the will and the codicil are inconsistent.

2.2 Who are the players?

All wills involve four different categories of people: a testator, an executor, witnesses, and beneficiaries.

- A *testator* is the person who makes a will. In the past, prior to the adoption of gender-neutral language in the law, a woman who made a will was called a *testatrix*. Now, however, women and men are both called testators. After testators have died, they may be called *decedents*.

- An *executor* (called in some states a *personal representative*) is the person responsible for collecting a decedent's property, paying creditors, paying expenses of administration, paying any taxes due, and distributing the decedent's property to the persons who are legally entitled to it. Your executor can be someone you name in your will, or if you do not have a will or fail to name an executor, someone appointed by the court.

- *Witnesses* are adults who sign your will to verify that they actually saw you put your signature on it. Witnesses should *not* be people who will receive any of your property under the terms of your will. It is also best that witnesses not be relatives by blood or marriage. Witnesses should include their contact information (i.e., addresses and phone numbers) when they sign.

- *Beneficiaries* are the people who will receive your property under the terms of your will or under the terms of documents such as insurance policies or retirement accounts. Beneficiaries also may be called *heirs* if they are relatives who would be entitled to inherit your property if you did not have a will. Beneficiaries are sometimes called *devisees* if they do not qualify as heirs. **Note: Under the law, heirs are only those people recognized as your closest relatives. Therefore, nonrelatives are not your heirs, strictly speaking, even if they inherit something under your will. That is why it is better to use the term beneficiary, which includes both relatives and nonrelatives who will receive property under your will.**

2.3 Estates and their administration

There also are specialized words that describe how wills are handled after the testator has died.

- Your *estate* consists of all property you own, both "real" and "personal." (The difference between real and personal property is discussed in section **2.4** of this chapter.) Your estate can include land, houses, furniture, personal belongings, checking and savings accounts, business interests, investments, life insurance, retirement benefits, and anything else of value. It can include both the property you own by yourself as well as property owned jointly with someone else.

- *Estate administration* is the court-supervised procedure for transferring your probate property upon your death according to methods provided by the law of your state.

- *Probate* is the legal process for proving the validity of a will. Courts that handle this process often are called probate courts. The exact process for probate will vary depending on the law of your state. The word probate is also sometimes used more loosely to mean the same thing as estate administration.

- *Probate property* is property that is subject to estate administration. In other words, it is property that will be governed by the terms of your will or, if you do not have a will, by the laws in your state that distribute your property after you die. A good example of probate property is any property held in your own name only, such as your home or other real property you own by yourself. This kind of property passes to others under your will and is subject to estate administration.

- *Nonprobate property* does *not* pass to another person under your will, and it is *not* subject to estate administration. Rather, your nonprobate property passes to other people by some legal means other than your will. This most often occurs because your interest in the property ends at the moment of your death or because the property must go to some other designated person by law or by contract. Common examples of nonprobate property are life insurance payable to beneficiaries, some types of trusts or financial accounts for which you have designated a beneficiary, and real estate you own jointly with another person with "right of survivorship." (A survivorship right means that when one of the joint owners dies, the other joint owner automatically receives the entire property.)

- *Dying intestate* is a term used to describe a person who dies without a will. If you die without leaving a will, the court will appoint a personal representative, and your property will pass to those persons whom the law has designated. This is called the law of *intestate succession*. It also applies if your will neglects to dispose of all your probate property. In essence, the law of intestate succession makes presumptions about who should receive your property when you die. Generally, it favors your spouse or other close relatives, but it will distribute your estate to more remote relatives if you have no living close relatives when you die.

- *Lineal descendants* are people born in your direct bloodline. They are your children, grandchildren, great-grandchildren, and so forth. Lineal descendants are sometimes called *issue*.

- *Per stirpes* is a Latin term that means "by the root." It is used when a testator wishes to divide property equally among a class of lineal descendants, such as his or her grandchildren. This is often done when a testator's children, who are the parents of the grandchildren, have died. Under the per stirpes method, the estate is divided into shares equal to the number of children. Each grandchild then would divide equally among themselves the amount their dead parent would have received if alive.

   > **EXAMPLE:** Linn had two children, now both dead. Her son had only one child, while her daughter had two children. Linn's will, written before her children died, leaves her entire estate to her two children "per stirpes." As a result, the estate would be divided in two because she had two children. Her dead son's child would receive his father's entire share — one-half the estate. Her dead daughter's two children would divide their mother's share, meaning they each would get one-fourth of the estate.

- *Per capita* is also a Latin term, meaning "by the head." It describes another method of distributing property among a class of descendants. Under this method, each living member of the class would receive an equal share.

EXAMPLE: In the example, suppose Linn revised her will after her children died, and in the new will left her entire estate to her grandchildren per capita. Since she has three grandchildren, each would receive an equal one-third share. However, if one of the grandchildren died before she did, her estate would be divided equally between the remaining two.

- To *devise* is to give real estate away in a will. The act of doing this is also called *a devise*. Today, the word "give" is often used as a plain English substitute for devises and bequests (see below).

- To *bequeath* is to give personal property away in a will. The act of doing this is called a *bequest*. Today, the word "give" is often used as a plain English substitute for bequests and devises (see above).

- *Escheat* is a term to describe the situation when your entire estate is given to the state to do with as it likes. This happens if you die without a will and leave no heirs named in your state's law of intestate succession. In that case, you are deemed to have died without heirs, and your entire estate falls to the state. (In legal terms, your estate escheats to the state.) Although it is rare for people to die without having even remote heirs, this scenario does underscore the importance of having a will.

2.4 Types of property

Property rights fall into many different categories, and you should keep these categories and their differences in mind when planning your estate. They can be used to your advantage — or can cause your estate trouble if you fail to understand them.

As noted earlier, property can be either probate (that is, subject to a will) or nonprobate (that is, not subject to a will). (See Chapter 3 for more details.) But property, whether probate or nonprobate, also can fall into still other categories with differences that can have a major impact on estate planning. The two broadest categories are *real property* and *personal property*.

- Property is considered *real property* if it is land (real estate) and usually includes buildings or fixtures that are permanent parts of the land. Ownership is documented by deeds that can be found in public records or in other documents.

- Property is considered *personal property* if it is not real estate. Personal property has two subcategories: tangible and intangible. Personal property is considered *tangible* if it consists of objects like furniture, clothing, and motor vehicles (objects are sometimes called "movables" because they are easily moved from place to place). The ownership of tangible personal property may or may not be recorded, depending on what type of property it is. (For example, it is common for there to be no official record of ownership of furniture, but the ownership of automobiles is noted in official certificates of title.) Personal property is *intangible* if it is not an object but rather a legal interest in something valuable like stocks, bonds, bank accounts, life insurance, and contract rights. It is common for ownership of intangible personal property to be recorded in documents such as corporate or bank records, insurance policies, and written contracts. Most often these documents are worth a certain amount of money that can be paid only to named persons under particular circumstances. However, this is not true of "bearer bonds," which are payable to anyone who has physical possession of them.

See Chapter 3 for more information on property and estate administration.

3 Understanding Estate Administration and Property

1. Probate and Nonprobate Property

When you are writing your will and planning the administration of your estate, it is very important to understand the different ways probate and nonprobate property are treated under the law. Always remember that probate property is subject to the terms of your will, if you have one, or to the law of intestate succession if you do not. But nonprobate property will automatically go to another person when you die, and it is not affected either by your will or by the law of intestate succession. Put another way, probate property must go through probate court to be transferred to the persons entitled to it. But nonprobate property can be transferred simply by proving to the proper authorities that the person who owned the property has died. (See Chapter 2 to review the meanings of probate and nonprobate property.)

> **EXAMPLE:** George died owning 500 shares of valuable corporate stock. He owned 200 shares solely in his own name (a form of probate property) and 300 shares as a joint owner with a "right of survivorship" (a form of nonprobate property) with his sister Janet. His will leaves his entire estate to his brother, Tom, but makes no mention of Janet. In order for Tom to get his 200 shares, he would have to go through probate in court. His inheritance might even be reduced by any unpaid debts George owed. Janet, on the other

hand, would simply have to submit a few documents to a stock-transfer agent proving George's death to get her 300 shares. And she would get those 300 shares even though she is not named in the will.

Probate property, in other words, can involve more complex procedures and more delay than nonprobate. But that is not always a bad thing. The underlying purpose of probate is to ensure that your wishes are honored when your property is divided.

1.1 Advantages and disadvantages of the two forms of property

So should you arrange your estate to consist mostly of probate property or of nonprobate property? There is no one answer. Probate property often avoids some of the pitfalls to which nonprobate property can be subject. But there are also times when it works to everyone's advantage to put property into nonprobate forms. Lets consider two examples:

> **EXAMPLE:** John is a young unmarried man who has been diagnosed with Lou Gehrig's disease (amyotrophic lateral sclerosis, or ALS). Doctors say he probably will not live past another 18 months and that he will need daily care for a major portion of this time. Because John is childless, he wants to leave everything he owns to his only surviving parent, his loving mother, Belinda, who will soon come to care for him in his home. If for some reason his mother dies first, John wants to leave his property to the university he attended. His largest assets are his home and a substantial deferred compensation account he invested wisely in the stock market. John consults with a lawyer, who prepares a deed that puts the home in both John and his mother's name, with a right of survivorship. After talking with his employer's personnel office shortly before his disability retirement, John also changes his deferred compensation account so his mother is the named beneficiary. Finally, the lawyer prepares a will saying that if John's mother dies before him, his entire estate will go to his university.

By taking the steps in the above example, John has converted the bulk of his estate into nonprobate property, and he has ensured that his mother will receive the home and deferred compensation account quickly upon his death, without needless legal complication. In some states, the procedures he has used might even help shield his property from claims by his creditors if it did turn out that he had large uninsured medical expenses at the end of his life. He also has taken into account what will happen if his mother does not survive him. If she dies first, his home and bank account again would become probate property governed by the terms of his will and would eventually be given to his university after his debts were paid.

Now let's consider an example in which converting property into nonprobate forms would *not* be a good strategy:

EXAMPLE: Emily's husband died years ago. She and her husband had one child, Frank, who is now an adult. Worried about providing for Frank after her own death, Emily makes Frank co-owner of her home with a right of survivorship and turns her bank account into a joint one in which either she or Frank can sign for the money. She makes this change so Frank will be able to pay her expenses in her declining years. But two years later, Emily meets the man of her dreams and remarries. She now wants to leave her property to her new husband when she dies. But Frank refuses to give up his joint ownership of either her home or her bank account. In the argument that follows, Frank marches into the bank one day and removes all the money from Emily's account. Emily is devastated, but the bank says it can do nothing since Frank lawfully could remove the money from an account he jointly held.

In this example, Emily's decision at first seemed to make sense. What she failed to consider, however, was that her relationship with her son might change in unpredictable ways. Converting property into nonprobate forms often carries this kind of risk, so many people prefer to retain sole ownership of property whenever possible and use their wills to dispose of property on their deaths. A will does not create any present ownership rights;

it simply dictates who will get ownership after the testator's death. In addition, a testator can change his or her will easily and at any time. Though Emily may not have realized what the future held, it would have been wiser for her to retain complete control of her property and simply leave it to Frank in a will. After her relationship with her son soured, she then could have changed her will in favor of her new husband *whether or not* her son agreed. And she never would have lost the money in her bank account.

As you can see, when it comes to estate planning, there are advantages and disadvantages involved in each way of owning property. Advice from a professional can sometimes be crucial to avoiding mistakes and minimizing the risks involved in changing methods of ownership. In John's case above, the risk involved in putting his property into nonprobate form was probably worth taking due to his serious illness and the desire to transfer his property to his caregiver mother quickly and with the fewest liabilities. Transferring in a nonprobate form can greatly reduce or even eliminate the costs of estate administration, which can literally take money away from your heirs. But Emily's case showed an instance in which the risk was not worth taking because of events she could not have predicted. Note also that John was careful to merely name his mother as the beneficiary of his deferred compensation account — something he could change at any time whether she approved or not. Emily could have done something similar with her bank account, but instead she foolishly gave an untrustworthy son power over the account equal to her own. Her entire problem might have been avoided if she talked first with a trained professional.

1.2 Keeping track of probate and nonprobate property

As you perform your inventory of your estate, you'd be wise to determine which of your possessions are probate property and which are nonprobate property. Always remember that probate property will go to other people under the terms of your will (or under the law of intestate succession if you do not have a will). Nonprobate property will pass under the terms of the documents that govern it.

As the previous examples suggest, whether your property is probate or nonprobate can make quite a difference to your estate. It is worth your time to pay careful attention into which category your property falls, especially in those instances in which you have a choice. For example, the proceeds of a life insurance policy or deferred compensation account would be nonprobate property if you have designated a beneficiary. The proceeds would be paid directly to your beneficiary and may avoid being reduced by claims of your creditors. But if you have failed to designate a beneficiary or the beneficiary you've named has died, the proceeds would be considered probate property. They would be paid to your estate and could be used to pay off your outstanding debts. That is why it is very important to include insurance policies, jointly owned property, and financial accounts in your inventory of your estate. You especially need to keep track of who you have named as beneficiaries and whether these designations need to be updated. If you don't remember who you have designated as beneficiaries, you can check this out by contacting whoever maintains the records. For instance, the insurance company would maintain records about beneficiaries of your insurance policies.

Another way to make property nonprobate is by creating a trust. When properly drafted, a trust can help you avoid some federal or state estate taxes. Such taxes apply to substantial estates, so trusts are normally useful only if there is a good chance the estate will be large enough to be taxed. Trusts can also be useful if there is a need to have your estate managed on behalf of your beneficiaries. People who want to create a trust should obtain the advice of trained professionals in their own states. (See Chapter 4 for a more detailed discussion of trusts.)

For many years, the threshold for federal taxation of an estate was $600,000, but the law has changed so that this amount will rise until it reaches the $1 million level in 2006. (See Table 1 in Chapter 4.) Anyone with an estate large enough to meet these amounts must get professional help from lawyers, accountants, and others. Tax law is complex, state taxes on inheritances vary widely, and large estates can involve legal issues beyond the scope of this book.

2. The Special Considerations of Jointly Owned Property

Property can be jointly owned by several people, and jointly owned property can be either probate or nonprobate, depending on the circumstances. It can be a useful tool in estate planning, but it can also pose special problems.

2.1 Tenants in common

Tenants in common is a form of joint ownership involving two or more persons, each owning an "undivided interest" in a property. In other words, the property has not actually been divided into separate parcels; all owners simply hold a percentage of the undivided whole. For example, if you own a house as a tenant in common with someone, you don't own just the upstairs of a two-storey house while the other person owns the downstairs. You both own half of *all* of the house. Real property is frequently owned this way. For instance, a deed may read "To Troy Monroe and Michael Monroe, each an undivided one-half interest, as tenants in common."

Property held as tenants in common is considered probate property. Upon the death of a tenant in common, the deceased tenant's share passes according to his or her will, and is subject to estate administration. If there is no controlling will, that share is subject to the laws of intestate succession. The decedent's share does *not* pass to the surviving joint owner automatically, and complications can arise because of this.

> **EXAMPLE:** Troy and his brother Michael owned a lakefront cottage they inherited jointly from their father. They held it as tenants in common, and their two families used the cottage for family reunions and other outings held many times a year — a family custom for three generations. The two brothers had informally agreed that the cottage would remain in the family so that future generations could enjoy these gatherings. After Troy's wife Anne died, Troy changed his will to leave everything he owned to his only child, Maria. Two years later, Troy died suddenly of a heart attack. When the estate was settled, Maria demanded that she be paid her half of the cottage's market value, but her uncle Michael did not have enough cash to meet Maria's demand. Maria hired a lawyer and successfully sued her uncle for a court-ordered sale. Unfortunately, the lawsuit itself cost Michael and Maria nearly a third of the total value of the cottage, leaving only the remainder to be divided between them. Bitterness over the lawsuit also sharply divided the family, leaving Maria, her husband, and her children permanently estranged from her uncle and his family.

Was this what Troy wanted? Probably not. Perhaps he thought his daughter would want to continue being part of the family reunions and would ensure that the lakefront property remained in the family for this purpose. But by leaving his half interest in the cottage to her, Troy gave Maria a right to do whatever she wanted with her share. When he drafted his will, Troy probably never even thought his daughter one day might want to sell the cottage. But the fact is that families can and do get into disputes over inherited property. If Troy's real purpose was to maintain family unity, other methods of ownership might have served his purposes better. At the very least, an attorney skilled in probate law might have been able to help avoid the problems that eventually arose.

2.2 Joint ownership with right of survivorship

When two people jointly own real estate with a right of survivorship, ownership automatically passes to the survivor when one of them dies. In the example above, Michael automatically would have become sole owner of the lakefront cottage when Troy died *if* he had had a right of survivorship. This would have been true even though Troy's will gave everything he owned to his daughter Maria. Troy's ownership interest would have ended at his death, and Maria would have had no right to half the value of the cottage. In fact, the lakefront cottage would not have been subject to estate administration at all because it would have been nonprobate property, and Michael could have transferred the deed over to his own name simply by proving that his brother Troy had died.

Survivorship is often used as an alternative to probate, especially by married couples and others who own property jointly but want the survivor to receive full ownership when one of them dies. A right of survivorship can be especially important to unmarried couples, because it can help them avoid the possibility of a challenge to the will by relatives. Survivorship also simplifies the process of transferring property after death.

> **EXAMPLE:** Gordon and Dee met and married each other late in life, after both their spouses had died and their children were grown. They decided to buy a small house together, with both contributing half the cost. Both had wills leaving their estates to their respective children, but they wanted to make sure that the small house itself would go to the survivor if one of them died. So, when the deed to the house was prepared, Gordon and Dee asked the title company to make sure it included survivorship rights. Now, when one dies, the other automatically receives full ownership of the house.

As with any form of joint ownership, there are risks involved in survivorship, the most significant of which is that of the joint owners having a falling out. But there can be other risks, too, especially for those who do not plan for unforeseen possibilities. Always keep in mind that any kind of nonprobate property, including property with a right of survivorship, can be suddenly turned into probate property by unexpected events. That is why you need to make and update your will even if you have converted some or all of your property into nonprobate forms.

> **EXAMPLE:** Karen and Leonard married each other after both had divorced their first spouses. Two years into the marriage, Karen gave birth to a son. Though Karen and Leonard had kept their other property separate, after the baby was born they decided to buy a new house, with the deed granting survivorship rights. Karen and Leonard had separate wills, executed shortly after their marriage, but each had named different beneficiaries and different executors. They did not update their wills after purchasing the jointly owned home, because they thought the survivorship right would take care of any problems. Tragically, while on vacation, Karen, Leonard, and the new baby were killed in a jetliner crash. Within weeks, a potentially costly dispute arose between their two estates over ownership of their home and its contents, since their two wills were not consistent with one another.

This is an example of a nonprobate strategy that failed. Since both Karen and Leonard died in the same accident, which one of their estates should have control over the house? Their mistake was failing to update their wills as their circumstances changed. Many states have laws to help sort out such problems, but that sorting out can become expensive.

Proper estate planning can eliminate many problems like this. It is common for wills to say what happens if a beneficiary of the will dies at the same time or shortly after the death of the testator (often called "simultaneous death"). In the case of married couples with separate wills, it is crucially important that the two wills be consistent with each other.

2.3 Tenants by the entirety

Tenants by the entirety is a unique form of joint ownership with survivorship rights, and it is available only to married couples. Property held this way falls into the nonprobate category: on the death of the first spouse, the property automatically passes to the surviving spouse. The one critical element of a tenancy by the entirety is the marriage of the joint owners. If they are not married or if their marriage is invalid, they will merely be tenants in common.

2.4 Life estate

The term "life estate" describes a situation in which a person owns an interest in property, but that interest ceases to exist the moment he or she dies. In other words, when the owner of the interest dies, the remaining ownership rights (called the "remainder") will go to the person named in the deed.

Life estates are used to create nonprobate property (for instance, when parents want property to go automatically to a child on their deaths without that property being subject to probate). Life estates also are used to let a surviving spouse live in and use a home for life, with the property automatically going to surviving children once the surviving spouse dies. For the reasons noted in the discussion about survivorship interests above, the use of a life estate as an estate-planning tool poses serious risks. Once a life estate is established, it cannot be ended without the consent of both the life owner and the owner of the "remainder," which can cause problems if these two people have a falling out or cannot agree on how to use the property. You should carefully consider these risks with help from trained professionals before you attempt to use a life estate in your own estate planning.

2.5 Joint bank accounts

Bank accounts can be put into joint ownership forms that make them nonprobate. These forms can range from limited all the way to unrestricted joint ownership, which can be a frequent source of trouble in estate planning and probate of wills. Unlike other forms of joint ownership, any single "owner" of a joint bank account can remove money from it, even if other owners do not know or consent. And creditors can sometimes try to access funds in the account to pay the debts of any one of its "owners." This poses obvious risks that make unrestricted joint accounts less attractive for estate-planning purposes.

However, there are ways of avoiding some of these problems. Some financial institutions will help you set up a POD (payable on death) account, or a "totten trust", or ITF (in trust for) deposit account. These types of accounts remain under your control for your life, with any funds in those accounts then going to your named beneficiary upon death. Make sure you read the exact terms of the documents the financial institution prepares, however, to ensure they reflect what you intend. And when you seek professional help from your bank or financial institution, be sure to tell them if your only goal is to set up a joint account that you completely control but that would be paid to someone else only when you die. Banks usually will help you set up these accounts at no cost other than normal account fees.

2.6 Community property

In a few states, married couples have a special joint interest in property obtained during the marriage called "community property." In most instances, community property includes money or property obtained by either spouse during the marriage, but excludes property obtained before the marriage or gifts made solely to one of the spouses.

Community property issues can complicate estate planning because the husband and wife actually own the property jointly, even if it is titled in only one of their names. The same can be true of money earned during the marriage or things purchased with that money. Furthermore, community property does not normally include a survivorship right — meaning it does not automatically go to the other spouse when the first dies. Issues about community property can require that the wills of both spouses be carefully drafted with professional help. There are nine community property states:

- Arizona
- California
- Idaho
- Louisiana
- Nevada
- New Mexico
- Texas
- Washington
- Wisconsin

Also keep in mind that property or money can keep its community property status even after you have moved away from one of these states. Problems also can arise if your will tries to deprive your spouse of her or his share of the community property you own.

3. Jointly Owned Property and Estate Planning

As discussed above, jointly owned property can pose special problems in planning your estate, especially if the joint owner and you disagree on how the property should be used either during or after your life. At the same time, some forms of joint ownership can be very helpful tools in estate planning. A right of survivorship, for instance, can quickly transfer real estate to your chosen loved one with a minimum of trouble.

Because there are advantages and disadvantages to joint ownership, it is always best to seek professional help on how to deal with any future problems that might arise. You should especially seek advice *before* you transfer wholly owned property into any form of joint ownership as an estate planning tool. There not only are practical pitfalls such as those noted above, but also possible tax problems. For example, you may be required to report the transaction to the Internal Revenue Service (IRS) as a "gift" if you do not receive fair market value for the transfer (see Chapter 4). Always remember that it pays to plan ahead and to ask for professional advice in these matters.

4
Trusts and Gifts as Estate Planning Tools

Both trusts and gifts can be used in estate planning to avoid estate taxes and to simplify or eliminate probate. But both trusts and gifts pose particular challenges and must be planned and managed carefully.

1. Trusts

Trusts are special arrangements in which the owner of property (usually called the trustor, settlor, or grantor) gives it to another person (the trustee or custodian) to manage on behalf of a third person (the beneficiary). It is even possible for the person who gives the property to be both trustee and beneficiary, thus filling all three roles at once. You can use trusts in your estate planning to —

- avoid state or federal estate taxes for large estates;

- provide for a child's future needs, such as educational expenses;

- set up a way to manage your property if your health is failing; and

- manage assets for someone who cannot do so for himself or herself.

Trusts can range from the very simple to the very complex. For example, you may establish trusts for your children, especially to meet educational expenses later in their lives. Such trusts are formed under a law called the Uniform Transfers to Minors Act and are often set up by a financial institution or investment firm at little or no cost, apart from the initial investment and regular service fees.

EXAMPLE: Gwendolyn's only daughter had a son, Chad. Shortly after Chad's birth, Gwendolyn took $3,000 and asked her investment counselor to put it into stock-market funds. Gwendolyn made her daughter custodian (trustee) of the fund under the Uniform Transfers to Minors Act. By the time Chad entered college, the fund had grown to more than $20,000, and his mother used it to help pay for a significant number of his educational expenses.

Gifts made under the Uniform Transfers to Minors Act usually remain in trust until the beneficiary reaches age 21. At that time, anything remaining in the account automatically goes to the beneficiary.

You also can use trusts to provide for adults who are unable to care for themselves.

EXAMPLE: Helen inherited a large sum of money from her late husband, and she wants all of it to go to her son, Peter, when she dies. However, Peter is developmentally disabled and unable to care for himself or manage his assets. After consulting professionals, Helen transferred her assets to a trust that she will manage as trustee for the remainder of her life. The trust property remains hers to do with as she likes. But after she dies, the trust will be managed for Peter by other people whom Helen trusts and will be used to pay for Peter's care and support. Most important, the trust will not have to go through probate, which means that the money for Peter's care will not be interrupted by legal proceedings or a challenge to Helen's will.

The above is an example of one of the more complex kinds of trusts, often called a "living trust," or in legal terms, an "inter vivos trust." It is one of many creative ways to use trusts in estate planning to properly manage assets.

Management of assets also can be a concern in your own lifetime if you are in declining health.

> **EXAMPLE:** Daniel is elderly and his health is beginning to fail. He has a son but does not trust him to manage property and money if Daniel loses the ability to do so himself. Therefore, Daniel has his attorney create a trust that will be professionally managed by a financial planner Daniel has chosen. If Daniel loses the ability to manage his estate, the financial planner will do so until Daniel dies. Any remaining property then will be given to Daniel's son under the terms of the trust.

Trusts are also useful for avoiding probate, which may be a special concern if you fear your will may be challenged in court, which would tie up assets needed to provide for your loved ones. Always remember that property in an estate is not actually distributed until the judge allows it. If a will is challenged, the assets might not be distributed for months or even years. But trusts can be used to minimize the danger of delay:

> **EXAMPLE:** Eileen has lived for more than 20 years with her life partner, John. Her estate consists mainly of a home, now worth $250,000, which she wants John to receive on her death. But Eileen's brother, Harrison, has always disapproved of the fact that Eileen and John never married and he is likely to challenge any will Eileen writes. As a result, Eileen consults an attorney, who creates a "revocable living trust" and transfers ownership of Eileen's home to the trust. Under the trust, Eileen still controls ownership of her home during her lifetime and can even change the terms of the trust if she wishes. However, the trust provides that on Eileen's death, John will be the sole beneficiary of the trust property. When Eileen dies, her brother will be unable to challenge the trust as he could a will.

Trusts can also be structured to reduce estate taxes, either by the creation of a living trust or through a "testamentary trust" — one created by your will. Normally, such a step is useful only if your estate is substantial. A trust would not be useful for tax purposes if your estate is small. Until 1999, no taxes were owed on estates worth $600,000 or less. This minimum amount will rise until it reaches $1 million in the year 2006. (See Table 1.)

TABLE 1
ESTATE TAX LIMITS

Year	Estate will be taxed if larger than:
2000-01	$675,000
2002-03	$700,000
2004	$850,000
2005	$950,000
2006 and beyond	$1,000,000

The minimum levels shown in Table 1 can be higher if the property involved qualifies under federal tax law as a family farm or a family business. This is of special importance because farmland or a business's inventory might have to be sold to pay estate taxes. However, the law in this area is very complex. You should get the advice of a trained probate lawyer if your family farm or business is worth more than the amounts shown in Table 1, as there are ways you can reduce taxes or restructure your property or estate plan to qualify you for the higher minimums.

It is possible for people with substantial wealth to use carefully created trusts to reduce the taxes their estates would owe. It is also possible to reduce taxes on an estate by making life insurance policies and similar assets payable to a trust.

However, creating trusts of this type — and planning for large estates — always should be done with professional advice. Though trusts are useful, they can also pose problems. In some instances, trusts must file separate tax returns. In addition, federal and state tax laws are constantly changing. In the year 2000, Congress began seriously considering new laws that would greatly alter or even eliminate estate taxes, so make certain you keep on top of any changes in the law. If the federal estate tax is eliminated entirely, you might need to reconsider your use of trusts as an estate-planning tool.

2. Gifts

One of the most useful estate-planning tools is also the most democratic of all: you can simply give property to others during your lifetime, rather than waiting until you die. Be aware, however, that gifts can bring tax consequences with them. Gifts may be taxable, though the law governing the gift tax is complex. Over the course of your lifetime, the federal government will keep a running total of gifts you give that have values above certain minimum limits. This amount may be taxable during your lifetime if your gifts are substantial, or when you die if your estate is large enough. Gift taxes and estate taxes are "unified" under federal law, which means the taxes are based on the total amount of your gifts, whether you make these gifts before or after you die, and whether or not you do so in a will. Because of this, tax problems are a major concern in estates that exceed the minimums, and this is also why some people use trusts to avoid probate (see section 1. earlier in this chapter).

The law does contain major exceptions that make the following gifts nontaxable:

- Tuition or medical expenses you pay for someone else
- Gifts to your spouse
- Gifts to a political organization
- Gifts to charities

- The first $10,000 of any other gifts you give to a single person in the same calendar year

This last category is the one most likely to create problems, but if your estate is likely to be taxed, it is also a very effective estate-planning tool. Under this exception, you can give up to $10,000 per year to any single person without creating any federal tax problems for yourself or your estate, now or in the future. In addition, the number of people to whom you may give is unlimited. For instance, if your estate is large, and if you have five adult children, you could give each of them $10,000 in cash per year. That would total $50,000 per year. Over a ten-year period, you could give these same five children $100,000 each, which would reduce the value of your estate by $500,000, and which would, in turn, greatly reduce the taxes that would be imposed on your estate.

Gifts, in other words, can help you address the problem of estate taxes. As long as you do not exceed the $10,000 exception, you do not have to file a gift tax return form with the IRS.

Consider an example for the year 2001, in which the first $675,000 of an estate's value is nontaxable:

> **EXAMPLE:** Jason died in 2001. His estate would have been worth $1 million that year *except for* nontaxable gifts worth $325,000 he had made to his children over many years. These gifts reduced the value of his estate to $675,000 at the time of his death, which he left in equal shares to his children. No tax was due because the first $675,000 was not taxable in the year 2001.

Note: Congress has authorized the $10,000 exception to be adjusted for inflation under certain circumstances in the future. Be sure to check the IRS forms to see if the amount has been adjusted.

The value of the $10,000 exception is doubled for married couples. Under what is called "gift splitting," a husband and wife can *jointly* give up to $20,000 to any single person without the gift being subject to tax. It does not matter which spouse actually makes the gift, so long as both agree to it:

EXAMPLE: Michael gives his son a gift of $20,000. That same calendar year, his wife Terri gives their daughter a gift of $20,000. Each knows about and agrees to these gifts. And though the gifts exceed $10,000 for each child, they qualify for the gift-splitting exception because the law treats these gifts as though each spouse gave half.

Gift splitting, however, does create more paperwork. The law says that both the husband and the wife must consent. To enforce this provision, the IRS requires that the couple file a tax form showing their joint consent, even if the amount qualifies as a split gift. This extra paperwork is the reason why many married couples prefer to each give separately no more than $10,000.

Apart from gift splitting, you must also file a federal gift tax form if you give more than $10,000 in gifts to any one person per year. You will not owe federal gift taxes, however, until the total amount you report to the IRS *over your lifetime* exceeds the amount shown in Table 1 (see section **1.** earlier in this chapter). In 2006, that amount will reach $1 million, which emphasizes the importance of gift giving as an estate-planning tool for people with significant wealth.

The unlimited exception for gifts to spouses is significant. Keep in mind that you can use this exception either for gifts during your lifetime or for property or money you give to your spouse in your will.

EXAMPLE: Harrison's estate was worth $2 million when he died in 2001. His will divided $675,000 of the estate equally among his children and gave the remaining $1,325,000 to his wife Yvette. The gift to his wife is nontaxable in its entirety under the marital exception. And the $675,000 left to his children equals the amount that is nontaxable. His estate would not have to pay any federal estate taxes.

The unlimited exception for spouses also applies to family farms and family businesses.

Finally, there are a few other important points you should keep in mind when thinking about using gifts for estate-planning purposes. First, a gift can include property that you transfer for less than fair market value:

> **EXAMPLE:** Winona owns many acres of land around her homestead. She wants her daughter, Joyce, to be near her, and so she gives the daughter two acres on which to build her own house. Joyce paid only $10 for the land, which is actually worth $20,000. As a result, Joyce has been given a gift worth more than $10,000, which she must report to the IRS.

Also, gift tax forms must be filed if you give anybody a future interest in property. You likewise must file a return if you give your spouse a property interest that will end when a certain event occurs. For example, you would have to report giving your spouse a life estate in property because your spouse's interest will end at her or his death.

Keep in mind that filing a gift tax form does not necessarily mean you owe taxes on your gifts. You are required to file the form so the federal government can keep a running total of nonexempt gifts you made during your lifetime. You can be penalized if you do not file reports when required.

Some states also impose gift taxes, and this should be taken into account before you make any gifts as part of your estate-planning strategy. Consult an accountant in your state to make sure you are aware of the tax consequences and pay any tax due.

5 Your Will: A Family Affair

amilies hold a special place in the law of wills. Most people sign wills leaving their property and money to people related to them by blood or marriage, and the law of intestate succession favors these same relatives when people die without wills. The laws in many states also give special protection against close family members being disinherited. You need to keep all this in mind when you decide how much of your property you intend to leave to your family members — especially if it is your intention to leave a significant part of your estate to people *not* related to you by blood or marriage.

1. Providing for Your Spouse

1.1 Minimum inheritance

It is usually impossible to completely disinherit a lawful spouse. In almost every instance, state laws say that your surviving spouse is entitled to a minimum amount of the estate, often called an "elective share". The exact amount varies from state to state, but is usually in the range of 30 percent to 50 percent of the estate. If your will does not meet this minimum, your spouse can go into probate court and overrule the exact terms of your will. Therefore, it is unwise to deliberately try to leave your spouse less than the law provides. Doing so can prolong the probate process, increasing probate costs and reducing the amount your beneficiaries will ultimately receive.

If you do have a reason to leave your spouse less than the minimum, you *must* get professional advice. In some states it is possible to reduce the amount of the elective share by converting property into nonprobate forms. But the law in this area is complex. It is also changing in some states and your estate may have tax problems if the work is not done properly.

1.2 The consequences of divorce

If you have a divorce pending, special problems can arise. You should ask your divorce lawyers if you need to take special precautions before your divorce is final. In some instances, it might be possible for your spouse to take a substantial portion of your estate if you die before the divorce is final, even if this is not what you wish. Your divorce lawyer may be able to minimize this risk by preparing a "divorce will" that will remain in effect until your divorce is final.

Also, keep in mind that you will need to make out a new will after the divorce, especially if your existing will actually names your former spouse. Although many states have laws that can prevent former spouses from inheriting under a will that was signed during the marriage, you still need to decide who should get the property you had planned to leave to your former spouse. Failure to update your will in these circumstances sometimes leads to property being distributed as though you had no will at all.

However, there are circumstances in which a person may want to leave money or property to a former spouse, especially if there are children from the marriage. If this is your situation, you will need a new will to avoid the state laws that otherwise might prevent your former spouse from inheriting this property.

1.3 Planning together

It sometimes happens that a husband and wife die simultaneously in an accident, or occasionally spouses die of unrelated causes within a few days of each other. If both spouses agree on who should get their property in either of these situations, both their wills should reflect their feelings. It is very important that the wills of the spouses not conflict with one another; otherwise, substantial cost and delay can result.

> **EXAMPLE:** Ken was a single man without children when he met and married Marcia, who had two children from a previous marriage that ended when her first husband died. Together, Ken and Marcia later had a son, Adam. Marcia never changed the will that she signed during her first marriage. It left all her property to "my children" if her first husband was dead, and it designated her former brother-in-law as the children's guardian and her executor. Ken, meanwhile, signed a will after Adam's birth leaving everything he owned to Adam and designating Adam's grandmother as guardian and executor in the event that Marcia was dead. Tragically, Ken and Marcia died together in an automobile accident. Almost immediately Ken's mother and Marcia's former brother-in-law began feuding over the inconsistent terms of the two wills. Their major fights were over custody of the children and how to divide Ken and Marcia's property between the two estates. The resulting legal problems were not settled for years, resulting in huge expenses and depriving the children of resources they otherwise would have had.

As this example illustrates, a husband and wife must work together to ensure that their wills are as consistent as possible. Marcia's biggest mistake was not updating her will, but she made other mistakes, too. Her will used the vague term "my children," without actually naming them. Thus, her son Adam — even though he was born years after the will was signed — apparently was lumped together with her first two children. But Ken also made a mistake: he should have worked with Marcia when he prepared his will after Adam was born.

A common mistake husbands make is to assume that they are the only ones who need a will or need to keep it up-to-date. That was true in an earlier day when the law gave husbands property rights over their wives, but today that is no longer the case. Good estate planning is always done jointly between a husband and wife.

2. Providing for Your Companion or Life Partner

Many people in the United States live together without being married. If this is your situation, and you want your companion to receive part of your estate, a will is especially important. This is true even in states such as Vermont, which now legally recognizes some life partnerships, and Oregon, which recognizes the right of some couples to inherit from each other even if they do not have wills.

2.1 State your intentions

Life partnership laws are new and largely untested. Having a will is a precaution well worth taking, since it could prevent your estate from being challenged by natural heirs such as blood relatives. It also is very important to include a statement in your will explaining your intention. For example, you might write —

> *I give my entire estate to my life partner, Mary Wilson. In doing so, I intend to disinherit all others. I specifically intend to disinherit all my relatives by blood and marriage because I have neither seen nor heard from any of them for more than 20 years and have come to regard them as strangers.*

There may be other situations in which two life partners are on excellent terms with their families. Or perhaps they do not intend to partially or completely disinherit their relatives by blood or marriage. Rather, they simply want to provide for their life partners. Consider the following sample language:

It is my intention to disinherit all persons, including members of my family and relatives by blood and marriage, to the extent they are not expressly provided for in this Last Will and Testament. In so doing, I do not diminish the genuine love and respect I feel for these persons, but only express my desire that my estate shall pass to those persons specified in this Will, under the terms specified, because the named parties have been a source of great comfort and assistance to me during my life.

Including language like this is important because the law still tends to favor relatives over all others, even if they are relatives you genuinely intend to disinherit. Giving a good reason for disinheriting relatives can help ensure that your wishes are respected in probate court. It also can discourage your relatives from trying to challenge your will in the first place.

Another tactic taken by some testators is to include a statement disinheriting anyone who challenges the will. Under the law, this type of statement is called an "in terrorem" clause. The Latin words mean "in order to frighten." Typically, the will leaves these people something of value but negates this gift if they challenge the will. In terrorem clauses are increasingly disfavored by the law, and many states refuse to enforce them.

2.2 Common-law marriage

In some states, a special problem can arise for a man and a woman who live together without getting married. Under certain circumstances, they can be regarded as being married to each other under a common-law marriage. This is not a limited form of marriage, but one with all the legal aspects of a marriage performed at a ceremony.

Common-law marriages date from a time decades ago, when in England and the United States it was common for men and women to cohabit — or live together — and simply act as if they were a married couple. If they did this and met certain other requirements, they were, for all purposes, regarded as married. Under this arrangement, each spouse was entitled to inherit property under the law in force in the state.

Common-law marriages can cause significant problems in estate planning, whether or not there is a will. Often, a court must determine that a common-law marriage actually existed, which itself can take time and cause expense.

Recently, there has been a trend to eliminate the legal recognition of common-law marriages. Most states now do *not* recognize a common-law marriage that supposedly came into existence within their own borders. However, some of these same states *may* recognize a common-law marriage that arose under another state's laws. Therefore, it is possible for a man and a woman to live together in a state that recognizes common-law marriages and still be regarded as legally married if they move to another state that does not recognize common-law marriages.

Also, you must keep in mind that common-law marriages could have come into existence many years ago, before a particular state abolished them. For that reason, it is a good idea to seek legal advice if you and a member of the opposite sex ever lived together as husband and wife but were not actually married in a ceremony.

In recent years, states that have recognized common-law marriages include—

- Alabama
- Colorado
- District of Columbia
- Georgia
- Idaho

- Iowa
- Kansas
- Montana
- Ohio
- Oklahoma
- Pennsylvania
- Rhode Island
- South Carolina
- Texas

The trend is to abolish common-law marriages, so some of the states listed above may have changed their laws by the time you read this book. *Check to make sure of the current law in your state.*

3. Providing for Minor Children

If you have minor children, having a will is crucial. When it comes to the welfare of your children, your will serves two vital purposes. First, it allows you to nominate someone to be your children's guardian after your death. Second, you can use your will and other estate-planning tools to provide financially for your children.

3.1 Nominating a guardian

Nominating a guardian for your children is important even if your spouse is alive. If both of you die at nearly the same time, your will is the best way for you to tell the courts who you think is best suited to be the guardian.

Carefully select a guardian who is a reputable and responsible person. A court normally will agree with your choice of guardian, but can disregard it if the person you name seems irresponsible or disreputable. In addition, you should talk to the person you choose for guardian in advance and make sure that he or she consents. A court usually will not force someone to become a guardian against his or her wishes. It also is wise to talk with your chosen guardian about your wishes for your children, such as their religious training and education. (See Chapter 7 for more details and sample clauses for naming a guardian.)

3.2 Financial considerations

A will also is important to provide for the needs of your minor children while they are growing. You might want your assets to be left to your children, but allow the adult guardian to handle the finances until the children come of age. Or, if you have substantial wealth or you want your children's assets to be professionally managed, you should seek advice from a lawyer and an accountant.

You might want to consider setting up a trust. Not only is a trust a very useful tool for distributing wealth to children and for potentially reducing estate taxes, it also provides detailed guidelines for managing the children's assets while they are growing. It is possible to create a trust while you are still alive (often called a living trust or inter vivos trust; see Chapter 4) or to create one under the terms of your will (often called a testamentary trust). A trust is also useful if you do not want your children to gain complete control over their inheritance when they reach a certain age. For that reason, a trust can be helpful even if you are not wealthy.

> **EXAMPLE:** Joan has a stock portfolio left to her by her late husband. She has let the portfolio grow so it will be able to provide for her only child, Jo Ellen, if Joan dies. But Jo Ellen is a rebellious 16-year-old, and Joan is worried that her daughter will not manage her inheritance wisely. An attorney has drafted a will for her that will transfer the portfolio to a trust managed by a professional who is also a close friend of Joan's. Jo Ellen's expenses will be paid from the trust, but she will not receive a final settlement from the trust until she is 25. Joan's will also nominates her mother as Jo Ellen's guardian if Joan dies before her daughter is of legal age.

Keep in mind that trust law is complex, and trusts can create tax problems. As a result, trusts need to be created with advice from professionals.

3.3 Property

Finally, you can also leave a specific item of property to your child in the care of an adult until your minor child reaches adulthood. Consider the following sample language:

> *I leave the German sword I confiscated from the enemy during World War II to my grandson, Harold K. Smith III, to be held by my son Harold K. Smith, Jr., until my grandson is of legal age.*

This type of clause in effect creates a kind of trust in which an item of personal property — in this case the sword — will be held for safekeeping by an adult until the child who is to receive it is older.

4. Providing for Grown Children

Of course, you can also provide for your grown children in your will. Sometimes parents wish to leave more to one child than to another. This may happen if one child is developmentally disabled or has other special needs. Or it may occur if a child is estranged from the parent. Consider the following sample language:

> *I have intentionally given nothing to my son, Michael Lucas, Jr., because I have neither heard from him nor seen him since he ran away from home in 1976.*

If you choose to leave nothing to a child, it is very important to expressly say why you are doing so, however painful this might be. *Simply failing to name that child in your will is not enough.* A child you thought you disinherited might convince a judge that you simply forgot about him or her, perhaps due to advanced age or illness. At the very least, failing to give a reason makes it easier for the disinherited child to challenge your will in court. The judge will want to know a good reason why you are disinheriting a child. You won't be able to give one yourself, because you will be dead. Only your will can speak for you.

Likewise, whenever you leave one child more property than another, it is best that you give a good reason for doing so. If you do not, the child who received less might be able to tie up your estate in court or persuade a judge to give him or her more. Consider this language:

> *I give my entire estate to my daughter, Helen Swain Watson. I am giving my only other child, my son, Dr. Madison R. Swain, nothing, because I previously paid his way through medical school and as a result he is now financially very secure.*

It is always a good idea to sit down with your children and talk with them about your will and the reasons why some may receive more than others. Talking it through while you still are alive may prevent them from challenging your will later. It will also give them a chance to voice any objections. Getting this kind of feedback may allow you to find out if one or more children intend to challenge your will despite your wishes. In that event, you should get the advice of an attorney in your state. Attorneys skilled in probate law can help you go over your reasons for leaving one child more than another and help you decide whether or not your reasons for doing so are worth the risk of a legal challenge to your will. Always keep in mind that, in some cases, challenges to your will can be expensive and could deprive your beneficiaries of a significant portion of their inheritance.

5. Family Farms and Businesses

Family farms and businesses receive special treatment under federal estate tax laws. This is of great importance to families who may have substantial wealth tied up in nonliquid assets like farmland or inventory. In some cases, beneficiaries have had to sell the farmland or business just to pay federal estate taxes.

You should determine if your family farm or business is worth more than the amount set forth in Table 1 in Chapter 4. If it is, consult with a probate lawyer to make certain you qualify for the special tax treatment and to take advantage of other ways to reduce the taxes that might cripple your farm or business.

Family businesses offer another useful option for estate planning. With help from professionals, these businesses can be used to set up retirement plans that will receive favorable tax treatment from the federal government. Plans of this type can help provide for your retirement *and* give your loved ones additional assets after you are gone. Retirement plans set up by companies are heavily regulated by federal law and should be created only with help from professionals.

6. Providing for Your Family during Probate

By its very nature, a will does not take effect until it has been probated or proven valid in court. This takes time. One important concern in estate planning is to ensure that your family or loved ones have enough income until the probate of your will is complete. There have been cases in which family or other loved ones have suffered a sudden loss of income and a diminished lifestyle until the estate was settled. If this may be the case for your family, you should consider ways to provide additional resources.

For example, you can arrange for life insurance payable directly to your beneficiaries. A supplement such as life insurance is especially important if you believe someone may challenge your will. In some instances, you also may be able to create a trust that will directly receive the benefits of a life insurance policy. It is possible to structure such a trust so that it is not considered part of your estate subject to estate taxes.

Another useful vehicle is a special type of Individual Retirement Account (IRA): the Roth IRA. An IRA is a form of deferred compensation. Money in an IRA usually earns interest without being taxed until the money is actually withdrawn. The major exception is the Roth IRA. Money in Roths is taxed when added to the account but earns interest over the years and can later be withdrawn tax-free. It is possible for IRAs and other retirement accounts to be set up to provide *both* for the people who created them and for their children or loved ones. These intergenerational IRAs are complex and should be created only with the help of qualified professionals.

Professionals also may be able to convert existing retirement accounts into an intergenerational form. In some ways, they operate like trusts, though they are heavily regulated by federal law. The law in this area too is changing constantly, which further underscores the need for professional advice. Nevertheless, intergenerational retirement accounts are an excellent estate-planning device. In some instances it may be possible to use them to provide significant income to a spouse, children, or other loved ones long into the future. Anyone who retires with a large sum in an IRA or other similar retirement account should consider using them.

6 Prepare Your Inventory

Now that you understand the basics of estate planning, you can begin the actual work. The most important step is to prepare an inventory of everything you own. As you do this, you should gather together the papers and information about your estate to verify your inventory. It is a good idea to put copies of all these papers in a single safe place and ensure that your executor knows where they are. For example, you might put all your papers into the same safe deposit box in which you plan to keep your will.

Once you've completed your inventory, sit down and talk with the person whom you would like to appoint as your executor. Doing so will give him or her an idea of the duties he or she might have to undertake. Always make certain this person agrees to be your executor. No one can be forced to be an executor against his or her will. Give your executor a copy of your estate inventory and make sure he or she knows where the original of your will is located and has ready access to it should you die.

Finally, keep your inventory up-to-date. Plan on doing a new inventory at least once a year; for instance, at the same time as you prepare your income taxes. Updating your inventory not only allows you to gather together new information your executor will need, but also helps remind you when your existing will needs to be revised.

Sample 1 shows an example of an estate inventory.

Note: If you are using this book a second time to make a new will or inventory your estate, make sure you have the most recent edition.

ESTATE INVENTORY

INVENTORY OF THE ESTATE OF

❧ Robert K. Jones, Sr. ❧

Today's Date: May 5, 2001

Personal Information

About You

Name Robert K. Jones, Sr.

Current Address 1411 N. Tropical Drive

Orlando FL 32801

Birthday November 14, 1940

Birth Place Pittsburgh PA

Social Security No. 555-55-5555

Military Service With U.S. Navy

Dates of Service: November 15, 1958 to November 15, 1961

Military Service No.: 5555555

Discharge Date: (same as above)

About Your Family

Current Spouse (if any) Helene Jones

Address 1411 N. Tropical Drive

Orlando FL 32801

Any Former Spouses? Marleen Watson Jones

(Give addresses) (died January 30, 1968; no children of this marriage)

Mother's Name ___Diana Jones___

    Address ___(deceased)___

    Birth Place ___Pittsburgh PA___

    Deceased & Date? ___died August 4, 1975___

Father's Name ___Harry Allen Jones___

    Address ___(deceased)___

    Birth Place: ___New York, NY___

    Deceased & Date? ___died May 8, 1955___

Your Children (Natural & Adopted), Their Addresses, & Birthdays

    Dara Jones Wilson, 511 W. 7th Ave., Orlando FL 32806 (born October 1, 1978)

    Robert K. Jones, Jr., 1411 N. Tropical Drive Orlando FL 32801 (born April 17, 1980)

Property You Own

Real Estate & Farms

Type	Location	Any Co-Owners?	Value
Home	1411 N. Tropical Drive	Helene Jones	$95,000
	Orlando FL 32801		

Businesses

Name	Type	Location	Any Co-Owners?	Value
N/A				

Business/Farm Inventory & Equipment

Name	Type	Location	Any Co-Owners?	Value
N/A				

Household Goods & Furniture

Type	Location	Value
Antique dining room suite from Thailand	(in my house)	$15,000
Living room furniture	(in house)	$1,200
Piano	(in house)	$500
Three bedroom suites	(in house)	$2,500
Kitchen appliances and furniture	(in house)	$1,500
Yard equipment	(in back yard shed)	$800
Clothing & linens	(in house)	$500

Motor Vehicles

Model	Year	Vehicle Identification Number (VIN)	Value
Honda Accord	1998	#55555555555	$10,500

Mutual Funds, Stocks, Bonds

Name/Company Number	Number of Shares	Value
N/A		

Bank Accounts & Certificates of Deposits

Name of Institution	Account Number	Value
Great American Bank	(checking) #45678456	about $2,600
Great American Bank	(savings) #64345234	about $5,000

Retirement Accounts, IRAs, & Annuities

Name/Company	Beneficiaries	Value
State of Florida Retirement Fund	my wife Helene Jones	$200,000

Life Insurance Accounts

Name/Company	Type	Beneficiaries	Value
DeSoto Insurance Co.	term life insurance	wife Helene Jones	$100,000

Other Property

Type of Property	Location	Value
Coin collection	Great American Bank safe deposit box	$1,000

TOTAL VALUE OF YOUR PROPERTY

$436,100

Debts You Owe

Mortgages

Type of Property	Location	Mortgage Holder	Amount You Owe
Home	1411 N. Tropical Drive	Great American Bank	$75,000

Credit Cards

Card Type	Account Number	Billing Address	Amount You Owe	Date
Discover	#555-55555-55555	(same as home)	about $5,000	May 11, 2001
Visa	666-66666-66666	(same as home)	about $3,000	May 11, 2001

Other Debts

Type	Lender	Address	Amount You Owe
Car loan	Great American Bank	Orlando	$5,400

TOTAL AMOUNT OF YOUR DEBTS:

$88,400

SUBTRACT DEBTS FROM VALUE OF PROPERTY

VALUE OF YOUR ESTATE IS:

$347,700

Part 2
Preparing Your Own Will

How to Make Your Own Will

1. The Requirements of a Sensible, Legal Will

Most people who make wills fall into a certain category — that is, they do not have substantial wealth and intend to leave their property only to immediate family members. This chapter explores the most common issues that affect wills of this type.

If your estate is not complex and is unlikely to be taxed or challenged by anyone, preparing your will need not be difficult. At its simplest, a will should —

- declare your intent regarding who will get your property when you die;

- meet certain formalities, including being written, signed, dated, and witnessed;

- contain evidence showing you understand what you are doing;

- name an executor and any alternate executors;

- take into account future contingencies, such as the possible deaths of beneficiaries.

Whether you wish to prepare your own will or have someone else do it for you, there are also certain considerations you must bear in mind about the form of the will. Some are required by law, and some are just recommendations for making a well-prepared will. These include the following:

(a) A will does *not* have to be written in any set form, but it is advisable to use the forms and language commonly used by lawyers. Several examples of typical language are shown in the samples in this chapter. (See Samples 2 and 3 and the sample clauses throughout this chapter.)

(b) A will must be in writing — either handwritten, type-written, or a combination of the two. However, it is always better to have your will typewritten, as doing so makes the will more legible. A will can't be a tape-recorded or videotaped statement, but you *could* video-tape the actual signing of the will to help prove your will is valid if the need arises. (See section **3.** on the next page.)

(c) A will must be signed and witnessed. (See sections **6.** and **7.** later in this chapter for more information.)

This chapter provides information on how to incorporate these requirements into your own will. Sample 2 shows a simple will with accompanying discussion that will be helpful to follow as you prepare your own will.

2. Holographic Wills

In a few states, a will is valid if it is written completely in the handwriting of the person who made it, provided the will is properly signed. These states typically accept the will as valid even if it is not witnessed. A handwritten will that is not witnessed is called a holographic will.

It is never a good idea to write a holographic will — even in those states that accept them — as legal problems often arise from them. For example, if there is any scratched-out or erased text, question can arise as to whether or not the text was scratched out or erased *after* the testator wrote it, which could result in the entire will being declared invalid.

Keep in mind, however, that a will does not become holographic merely because it is written out by hand. If the will is properly witnessed, it can be as valid as a typewritten will.

3.   Who May Make a Will?

All competent adults may make a will. In the United States, this normally means anyone 18 years of age or older. Minor children usually are not able to make a will, but there are exceptions. Courts sometimes give minors the rights of adulthood, and some legal acts can also do the same.

The most common example of a legal act giving a minor the right of adulthood is marriage. In some states, under limited circumstances, it is possible for minors to marry . Most commonly, older minors can marry with parental consent, or a judge can authorize a marriage based on evidence that the prospective bride is pregnant. In most jurisdictions, minors who are married are regarded as adults and, therefore, can make wills.

It is also possible for some minors in military service to make a will, especially those about to go into combat. If this is your situation, it is wise to discuss this possibility with military officers, since the government or the local bar association often offers to prepare wills of this type for free.

To make a valid will, you must also be competent or of sound mind. In legal language, you must have "disposing capacity" or "testamentary capacity," meaning that you are fully aware of what you are doing and that you are able to understand three things when you are preparing your will:

(a)   That you are making a plan to dispose of your estate after you die

(b)   The nature and extent of your estate

(c) Who the people are who would normally be your natural heirs

Further, your will must contain legal language specifically identifying the document itself as your last will and testament. This language includes the heading at the top of the document and an introductory sentence stating your intent. Lawyers present this information in many ways, but here is one common example:

I, Robert K. Jones, Sr., being of sound and disposing mind, declare this to be my last will and testament.

In this example, the first sentence gives the testator's full name, then notes that he is of sound and disposing mind. This is simply a common legal phrase meaning, "I know exactly what I'm doing here." Finally, the introductory sentence expressly identifies this document as Mr. Jones's last will and testament.

Problems can arise if there is reason to suspect that anyone making a will is mentally ill or suffers a serious impairment affecting his or her ability to reason, such as dementia, senility, or Alzheimer's disease. If there is a possibility you suffer from such a condition, you must consult with a lawyer about making your will. The lawyer may also want to have medical professionals examine you and witness the signing of the will and videotape the event.

A videotape could be useful if there is a possibility someone will challenge the will or if the testator has a disability that could call the will into question. For example, some states require special procedures if the testator has a disability that affects his or her ability to communicate, such as blindness or deafness. Or a testator may be in a final illness or suffer from a mental condition that hinders his or her ability to understand things. If any of these problems are present, it is important that you get the advice of a lawyer skilled in the laws of your state to make sure you minimize the risk of a legal challenge to your will.

Your will also needs to give away all of your property. If for some reason you fail to do so, it could be taken as evidence of memory loss or some other problem. If there are people unhappy with your will, they could use your failure to name all your property as evidence that your will is invalid. At the very least, such a situation would create a costly legal problem for your estate and could even result in the "forgotten" property being given to someone you do not want to have it.

Simple wills often get around this problem by stating that you, the testator, are giving away your "entire estate," which avoids the problems caused by attempting to list everything. If you then wish to give specific items of property to someone else, you can do so by adding a specific new language:

> *I give my entire estate to my wife Helene Jones. However, I give my 1968 Ford Mustang automobile (vehicle identification #555-55-5) to my son Robert K. Jones, Jr., in recognition of the time he spent restoring it.*

(Also see section **5.2** later in this chapter for information on writing specific bequests.)

Finally, proving an understanding of your natural heirs is not difficult. Lawyers routinely put a statement in wills, typically near the top, that simply recites the names of your closest family members. Consider this example:

> *My closest family consists of my wife Helene Jones, our two children, Dara Jones Wilson and Robert K. Jones, Jr., both now adults, and three grandchildren.*

This listing includes every living person who normally might be entitled to inherit from Mr. Jones when he dies.

4. Naming an Executor

The executor is the person appointed by you in your will to be responsible for settling your estate. Your executor's responsibilities may include paying any taxes due, settling unpaid debts (including unpaid funeral costs), collecting money owed to your estate by others, distributing your estate to your beneficiaries, and giving a final accounting to the probate court.

4.1 Choosing an executor

You should select an executor whom you know to be reliable and trustworthy. If your executor dies before you do and you neglect to update your will, a court could appoint someone else — even a stranger — to be your executor.

Your executor must be capable of fully exercising his or her legal rights. You may not appoint as your executor a minor or someone who has been legally declared incompetent, such as a person who has a legal guardian. You must also avoid naming someone as your executor who has an illness that might interfere with his or her ability to make decisions about your estate, such as a parent who has Alzheimer's disease or a spouse with a terminal illness. If your named executor is incompetent at the time you die, the court will not appoint that person as your executor and could, as above, even name a stranger to manage your estate.

It is common for people to name as their executor a family member who actually will receive their estates — unless, of course, that person lacks the ability to make decisions about the estate. Spouses often name each other as executors. Some people choose to name their children. Such arrangements minimize costs that the family otherwise might have to pay if someone else is chosen, and are most useful for smaller estates. An independent executor could be entitled to a fee paid out of the estate; an executor who is a beneficiary is entitled to a fee as well, but it is pointless for a family member to ask for a fee from the same estate he or she ultimately will receive.

Choosing an executor can be more complicated if there is the chance that someone may challenge your will or if you have a substantial estate. Keep in mind that taxes are a major problem in very large estates, and that it is absolutely essential that large estates be managed by people who know how to minimize the taxes that may be owed.

For practical and legal reasons, it is better to name as your executor someone who lives in your state, preferably within driving distance of your county. If your executor must travel long distances, the expense of doing so will be paid out of your estate. Some states also put special restrictions on out-of-state executors that could cause problems. (For example, a state may restrict out-of-state executors to family members or impose special obligations on them.)

Finally, as mentioned previously, you should not name someone executor of your estate unless he or she agrees to take on this responsibility. Courts will not force a person to be an executor if he or she does not want to be. It also is wise to talk with your executor about your will, your plans for your estate, and problems that might arise in settling your estate. Make sure you keep a copy of the inventory of your estate (see Chapter 6) in a place where your executor can readily find it when you die, so that your executor will have information about the extent of your estate and the location of your property as soon as it is needed.

4.2 Coexecutors

You may choose to name more than one person as your executor. In this case, the coexecutors share the duties of settling your estate. Such an arrangement helps divide the burden and can be helpful for families with smaller estates. Be aware, however, that disputes can arise, and that an argument between coexecutors may have to be decided in court. On the other hand, problems can also occur if you name only a single executor who then tries to take unfair advantage of his or her authority. For example, a child you name as your executor could try to divide property unfairly with brothers or sisters.

Every family is different, so the decision whether to have one executor or to appoint coexecutors is one you must make in light of your own circumstances.

4.3 Naming an alternate executor

Many wills name an alternate executor (or executors). This is someone who would serve in that role if your preferred executor is unable to do so for any reason. Keep in mind, however, that it is always best to update your will if anything happens to prevent your named executor from serving in that role (e.g., the person dies or becomes mentally or physically unable to serve). And it is necessary to update your will if this person simply no longer wants to be your executor or you no longer trust him or her. You never want an executor who doesn't wish to serve, or who may actually be hostile to you or your family's interests or those of your beneficiaries.

Naming an alternate executor is wise in any case. Suppose both you and your named executor die in the same plane crash, or your executor dies in a separate accident or medical emergency shortly after your death. It would be very important that your will named an alternate.

Here is a sample clause naming both an executor and alternate executors:

> *I name my wife, Helene Jones, as my executor. If she cannot serve, I name my daughter, Dara Jones Wilson, as my executor. My executor(s) shall serve without bond; shall have authority to appoint a successor, alternate, or coexecutor; shall exercise the fullest extent of authority allowed by law to an executor; and may administer my estate by any alternative method allowed by law.*

This sample clause first names the primary executor, Helene Jones. Then it names an alternate, the daughter. (If you wanted, you could name a whole string of alternates, but if you do so, be very clear about the priority in which they will serve.)

4.4 Defining the extent of your executor's power

In the sample language above, the last sentence gives the executor broad leeway to probate the estate. Some states may require an executor to post a good-faith bond before probate. If so, this may cause a problem if the amount of money that must be posted is too high. It is very common for wills to waive the bond requirement as a way of encouraging the executor to serve. The waiver may not always be honored by the judge, but it often is.

The sentence above also gives the executor authority to name a successor, alternate, or coexecutor. This authority is useful in dealing with problems that could arise if, for instance, your executor became too ill to serve, had to move far away for a job, or simply found that he or she could not fulfill the role.

Finally, the sentence above also indicates your desire to give your executor the broadest powers available by law and allows him or her to probate your estate by any alternate means available. In some states, there is more than one way to probate an estate, some methods being better suited for particular purposes. Giving the executor power to choose is important because it lets the executor make the choice that is best at the time.

It is possible to limit the executor's powers in a will, which is done in complex estates with special problems that would require a lawyer's help. Some famous authors, for example, may name two executors: one to handle legal matters associated with the books they have published, and another to handle other matters. Problems like these seldom arise in smaller, simpler estates, which are usually settled by a single executor with broad powers.

5. The Basic Clauses: The Importance of Exact Language

It is very important that you use exact language when you write your will. You must avoid any ambiguity. If anything in your will is unclear, you run the risk of it being challenged in court, which can cost time and money and result in heartache for your family. For example, avoid using a phrase such as, "I think I would like my children to receive . . . " because it leaves doubt as to your real intent. Do you really want to give them equal shares, or is this something you were just thinking about? Perhaps you had not made up your mind when you signed the will.

In most instances, a judge will enforce what he or she thinks you intended, but do not let a vague phrase in your will become the excuse someone needs to challenge it. If you have any doubts about language in your will, consult an attorney. The legal fee could save your loved ones much grief.

5.1 Naming people

Anyone you mention in your will, whether your executor or beneficiaries, should be identified by his or her full name, along with any other identifying information. For example, do not write that you are leaving your estate "to my children, in equal shares." You should actually write their full names as shown in Sample 2. You should also avoid inexact phrases such as, "I would like my children to receive my estate in equal shares." It is better to simply say, "I give my estate in equal shares to . . . ," then name the people and specify what or how much they should receive.

5.2 Specific bequests

If you plan to give away specific items of personal property in your will, you must identify them as clearly as possible. Include identifying marks, serial numbers (check these for accuracy), or the location of the item. Whenever possible, avoid vague references such as, "I give my sister Faye the gold necklace my mother gave me in 1965." What if no one remembers which necklace that is, and your jewelry box contains several?

Some wills go into great detail about giving specific items of personal property away, but others adopt a more democratic approach. Consider the following sample language from a will:

I give my personal jewelry, which is located in safe deposit box 302 at American State Bank, 45 State Street, Phoenix, Arizona, to my two sisters, Darlene J. Watson and Roberta G. Stapleton, share and share alike.

The phrase "share and share alike" is frequently found in wills. It indicates that the named beneficiaries should decide among themselves exactly how to divide property, even though — technically — they are entitled to equal shares. This language is especially useful when it would be hard to divide the property equally. In the example above, Darlene may want only the more valuable heirloom necklace that belonged to her great-grandmother and would be willing to let Roberta have the rest. The phrase "share and share alike" lets them reach the compromise that works best for them. Alternatively, they could decide to treat each piece of jewelry as having equal value and divide it all in equal numbers. They might even decide to have the jewelry professionally appraised and then divide it "equally" based on the strict dollar amounts in the appraisal.

Besides leaving specific items of personal property to certain people, you may wish to leave someone a specific sum of money. In this case, you can state the amount of the gift (e.g., "I give $5,000 to John Doe"). Understand, however, that naming specific amounts of money carries some serious risks. If your estate does not have enough ready cash on hand at the time of your death, your executor might be forced to raise it by selling other property that you intended to leave to someone else.

In settling estates, it is usual for specific bequests to get higher priority than other types of gifts. For example, suppose you leave a specific bequest of $5,000 to your daughter, but you intend your spouse to receive everything else, including your home. This would cause a serious problem if, at the time of your death, the only thing you own *is* your home. The specific bequest of $5,000 in cash could be given higher priority than your gift to your spouse, even though this is not what you intended. The result? Your spouse could lose the home in which you have lived, since it might need to be sold to pay the $5,000 gift to your daughter. Therefore, it is very important to be careful when making specific bequests of money. There would be no problem, however, if you gave a specific item of property that you know will be a part of your estate.

5.3 Thirty-day clause

One of the most important clauses to be included in your will is known as the "30-day clause." The will shown in Sample 2 has an example of such a clause, which comes into play if a beneficiary dies shortly after you do. Should that happen, then without the 30-day clause, your estate would have to go through probate twice: first as your estate and then as part of the estate of the person you named as your beneficiary.

This situation would not only needlessly complicate and delay settling your estate, but also could cause serious tax problems if your estate is large enough to owe federal or state taxes. The estate could be taxed twice. The 30-day clause is a simple device for dealing with this problem.

Note: There is no absolute requirement that the length of time be 30 days. It can be shorter or longer. But keep in mind that there is greater risk of a "double probate" if the time is shorter. And if the time is longer, the settling of your estate will be delayed for that period of time. If you set the period at a full year, for example, your estate could not begin probate until the full year had passed.

5.4 Residuary clause

Another special concern is that you include language in your will to make sure that you dispose of your entire estate. For example, some wills include detailed lists of property to go to particular people, but do not include property that was obtained after the will was written. A "residuary clause" can deal with this problem.

This clause simply says who gets the "residue," or the remaining property. The following is an example of a common residuary clause:

> *I give the rest, residue, and remainder of my estate to my daughter Lauren Esther Westmoreland.*

This means that the daughter will receive all other property that was owned by the testator and which was not given away somewhere else in the will.

Including a residuary clause is not absolutely necessary if your will expressly disposes of your entire estate, but it is still a good precaution. A residuary clause is also important if your will leaves property to someone who dies before you do. If you did not name an alternate to get this property, it would go to whomever you have named in your residuary clause.

5.5 Clauses related to minor children

Minor children pose a special challenge in estate planning. A single parent obviously must worry about who will take custody of the child if the parent dies, especially if the other parent is already dead. Even two-parent families must worry. What if both parents die in the same accident? What if you have divorced the child's other parent and have remarried? Would custody go to the stepparent or the natural parent? In some instances, it might be better for the child to remain with the stepparent; in others with the natural parent. Issues like these require serious thought.

First and foremost, your will should contain a clause nominating a guardian for all your minor children. And it is critically important that your spouse's will contains a clause nominating the same guardian so that there can be no question about whom you both want. You must agree. If your two wills disagree on the guardian, the judge would have to resolve the problem if both parents die simultaneously. It could result in a costly legal dispute if the two named guardians decide to challenge each other or, worse yet, try to split your children between them. The emotional toll on your children could itself be severe at a time when their entire lives have already been disrupted by the death of their parents. In fact, parents who care for their children are taking a huge risk if they do not have wills that include the nomination of a guardian. Although the nomination must still be accepted by the judge, it is always given great weight if your choice is obviously in the children's best interests. It is a way you can literally tell people after you have died who you want to care for your children.

Here is a sample clause for a married couple planning for the guardianship of their natural children, if they both die within a short time of one another:

[From the husband's will]

If my wife, Eileen Carr Strait, predeceases me, or if we both die simultaneously, I nominate my wife's sister, Helen Carr Burrell, as the guardian of my children, Tammi Strait and Jacob Strait, because of the love and affection Helen Carr Burrell has shown them from the time of their births and because they regard her as a second mother.

[From the wife's will]

If my husband, Jacob Harold Strait, predeceases me, or if we both die simultaneously, I nominate my sister, Helen Carr Burrell, as the guardian of my minor children, Tammi Lynn Strait and Jacob Carr Strait, because of the love and affection Helen Carr Burrell has shown them from the time of their births and because they regard her as a second mother.

Note how these two clauses coordinate perfectly with each other. Whether both parents die together or one dies first, the same result will be achieved. This would be true even if one was killed in an accident that mortally wounded the other one, who died weeks later. The guardian nominated is the same no matter how the sequence of events plays out. In this way, these parents have made sure there can be no uncertainty about their wishes for their children's care.

It is even more important to name a guardian if the other parent is already dead, especially if you do not trust your closest relatives to rear your children properly. You might consider a clause along the lines of this example:

> *Because my child's father Ernesto Suarez is dead and because I am estranged from the members of my own family and do not trust them to rear my son properly, I give my entire estate to my only child Roberto Suarez, and I nominate my sister-in-law, Adella Suarez Shaw, as my child's guardian until he is of legal age.*

More complicated problems can arise in naming a guardian for the children of divorced parents. As a general rule, if one of the parents dies, the other gets custody of the surviving children, even if the deceased parent's will named someone else as guardian. Courts are very unwilling to give custody of children to someone other than a natural parent unless there is a very good reason to do so. Simply stating in your will that you prefer someone else will seldom be enough. There have been bitter custody lawsuits between a surviving natural parent and others who view him or her as unfit to receive custody. Many unfortunate cases have involved grandparents who viewed their former son-in-law or daughter-in-law as an unfit parent and sued for custody of their dead son's or daughter's children. Most often, the grandparents do not win unless the surviving parent is truly unfit.

If you believe your former spouse to be an unfit parent for your mutual children, get the help of a lawyer to take whatever steps may be available in your state. For instance, if you have entered a second marriage, it may be possible for your new spouse to adopt your children by your previous marriage, which can give him or her custody rights superior to those of your former spouse. However, this move will typically require the consent of your former spouse. Nonetheless, it is a step worth considering. Your former spouse may be more willing to give up the children when you are still alive and healthy rather than when you have recently died. Some former spouses who have little interest in their children will sign the necessary papers. There may be other ways of terminating your former spouse's parental rights, but these will vary from state to state and will always require skilled legal help by an attorney.

Another consideration in dealing with children is who will manage the assets you leave them in your will. In most cases, that person will simply be the surviving parent or the guardian, especially if your estate is not large. However, larger estates and those that include investments such as stocks and bonds are more complicated, but there are many banks, accountants, and financial advisers who can help you set up a mechanism for managing these assets for your children. There are countless ways to manage assets, and some may be useful in some states but not others, depending on variations in state laws.

A trust also may be a very useful way of managing assets. It is even possible for one person to be your children's guardian, and another to be the trustee of the assets you leave them. Normally, your children will assume full legal control of assets you leave them when they become adults, but many parents do not want to give their children full legal control until they are older. If this is your situation, you can set up a trust that provides for a longer period.

6. Signing Your Will

Once you have written your will and are satisfied with all the details, you must properly sign it. You must sign the last page in the presence of witnesses. Most states require two witnesses, although a few require three. Having a third witness is a good idea, even if it is not legally required in your state, because it provides additional proof of your will's validity.

It is also recommended that each page of the will be initialed or signed by you and by the witnesses, in the presence of each other. This eliminates the possibility of someone substituting different pages in the will and serves as further proof that you reviewed the entire will.

You and the witnesses should not sign the will until you are all together in the presence of the notary public who will notarize your self-proof affidavit. (See section **8.** on the next page.)

There are some situations in which people may be unable to sign a will but can nonetheless verify it. It may be that a person has never learned to write, and for that reason, cannot sign his or her name. Usually such a person can verify the will simply by marking it with an X or any other mark. In this situation, it is doubly important that the witnesses know the person signing the will or receive proof of his or her identity.

In some cases, people lose the ability to sign their names due to disease or injury, but a will can usually be created by someone who is unable to sign as long as he or she can direct someone else to sign it and verify that it is his or her will. Problems can also occur for people with disabilities (such as blindness or deafness) that affect their ability to read or communicate. Some states may require additional proof that the testator has understood the contents of the will and has communicated that understanding to the witnesses. In these situations, it would be wise to consult with a lawyer to make sure proper legal measures are taken.

7. Witnesses to Your Will

The witnessing of your will is crucial. Without the proper witnesses' signatures, your will is invalid and has no legal effect. As stated above, the witnesses must watch you sign your will. Then they must sign the will in your presence and in the presence of each other and the notary public who will execute the self-proof affidavit. (See section **8.** below.)

It also is important to make sure that your witnesses are disinterested people who will not receive anything from your estate; that is, they should not be beneficiaries to your will nor should they be the spouses of beneficiaries. Your will is not necessarily invalid if a beneficiary serves as a witness, but this situation creates an opportunity for someone to challenge your will. Someone might argue, for example, that a beneficiary who signed your will as a witness had "undue influence" over you. (See section **9.**)

8. Self-Proof Affidavits

A relatively new idea in estate planning is to include a self-proof affidavit at the end of a will. This document is an affidavit (in other words, a sworn statement in writing, made before an authorized officer) by the witnesses that they did, indeed, witness the proper signing of the will and put their own signatures on it. (Samples 2 and 3 both contain self-proof affidavits.)

A self-proof affidavit is not a legal requirement of making a will in most states, but there are significant advantages to using one. Most states now recognize self-proof affidavits, and that means that the will is established as valid without having to call one or more of the witnesses into court to testify that it was properly signed. This speeds the probate process, eliminates the delay and cost of holding a court hearing, and protects the estate and its beneficiaries if the witnesses cannot be readily found.

It is worth using a self-proof affidavit even in those few states that do not recognize them. There is no penalty for using one, and doing so provides further evidence of the will's validity by showing that you understood the formality and importance of your will. As well, a self-proof affidavit provides yet another witness: the notary public, who can testify if needed.

Notary publics are commonplace in most communities, and many will notarize documents without charge. You can find a notary public near you by looking in the yellow pages of your phone book. Be sure to take photo identification with you, because many notaries will ask for proof of your identity before the signing begins.

9. Undue Influence

Your will must be the product of your own free will. If there is any evidence that it is not — that you were "unduly influenced" by someone else — your will may be challenged in court. Consider the following example:

> **EXAMPLE:** Georgianne inherited a lot of money from her father. Though she married several times, she never had children, but she doted on her grandniece Toni. Eventually she signed a will leaving everything to Toni. As Georgianne grew older and frailer, she came to depend more and more on her housekeeper, Margaret. One day Margaret told Toni that her great-aunt no longer wished to see her. At nearly the same time, Margaret told Georgianne that Toni had decided to cut off all contact with her great-aunt. Some months later, Margaret presented Georgianne with a new will and helped her sign it. Margaret and another servant were the only witnesses. The new will completely disinherited Toni and left all of Georgianne's money to Margaret. Three days later, Georgianne died. Toni later learned that Margaret paid a large sum of money to the other servant who witnessed Georgianne's will.

In this example, the grandniece, Toni, probably would be able to overturn the will because of the "undue influence" of the housekeeper, Margaret, owing to the following factors:

- Margaret's lies to Toni and Georgianne
- Margaret's being the source of the will and the one who helped Georgianne sign it

- Margaret's witnessing the will and paying off the only other witness

- Georgianne's lack of independent advice upon which she might have relied

- Georgianne's frailty and resulting dependence on Margaret

Most people would agree that a challenge to the will in this example would be fair. But there are problems here for well-meaning people who simply do not understand the law. Sometimes trying to "help" an elderly relative prepare a will can come back to haunt you.

> **EXAMPLE:** Harvey Johnson was a widower with two adult children, Dwain and Theresa. Dwain led a rebellious and wanton life, and often told people how much he hated his family. He had made no effort to see his father in years. Theresa, meanwhile, stayed with her father and took care of him as his health declined. One day Harvey asked Theresa to help him prepare a will because, even though he wanted Theresa to have everything, he was worried that Dwain might try to take half his estate. Theresa drafted a will for her father that left everything to herself and made no mention of her brother. When Harvey died, Dwain challenged the will on grounds his sister had undue influence over its creation. He argued that because the will did not even mention his name, his father was so mentally impaired that he had forgotten he even had a son and that Theresa took advantage of this situation. Ultimately, Theresa had to settle with her brother because the cost of his challenge to the will was eating up her father's estate. Each received less than half the estate; the rest paid for lawyers' fees and costs.

Though Theresa was well intentioned, her effort to help her father backfired. What could have been done to prevent this? The best strategy would have been for her father to hire an attorney to give him independent advice in creating his will. Her father wanted to disinherit her brother, which is an action that has a high risk of leading to a challenge of a will. The attorney could have helped make certain that the details of the will were what Harvey truly intended, apart from his daughter's wishes (and the up-front cost of consulting an attorney in this situation will almost always be less than the cost of a challenge after the testator is dead). It was also a grave mistake not to mention the son in the will. It would have been far better for Harvey to have included a clause such as, "I intend to disinherit my son, Dwain Johnson, because he has not visited me in many years and has shown nothing but disrespect to me for most of his life."

10. Revising Your Will

A valid will takes effect upon your death, no matter how long prior to death it was made. In the meantime, your financial position may have changed considerably for better or worse, so it is very important for you to review your will regularly and, if necessary, revise it. As mentioned earlier in this book, a good time to review your will is when you are preparing your income tax return; and as discussed in Chapter 2, there are several good reasons for revising your will, such as a change in the tax laws, a change in personal assets, the birth of a child or grandchild, the death of a named executor, or the death of a spouse, a child, or one or more of the people named in your will.

In many cases, if you want simply to change one or two clauses in your will, you can revise it by preparing a "codicil" instead of making a whole new will. A codicil is a supplement to an existing will and, when properly completed, becomes a legally binding part of the earlier will.

Suppose that when you make out your will, you give an item of property to one person, but later you decide to give it to someone else. Instead of changing the entire will, you can add a codicil that makes the change. Here is an example:

> *This is my codicil and is supplemental to my will dated the 12th day of July 2000. Paragraph 3 of my will, which*

gives my 1998 Toyota Sienna automobile to John Doe, now deceased, is hereby revoked. I hereby replace it with a new Paragraph 3 stating: "Allan Doe shall receive my automobile, a 1998 Toyota Sienna, vehicle identification #555-55-5."

The codicil must be signed by you, the testator, in the presence of witnesses in the same manner as a will.

As a general rule, it is better and less confusing to make a completely new will rather than to attempt piecemeal changes in a codicil. You make a new will in the same way as you made the first one. By making a new will you revoke the former one, which should be destroyed to avoid confusion, as your executor might mistakenly start to probate an earlier will if he or she simply has not yet found your more recent will. The most recent will is the one that becomes effective on your death. If your executor started to probate the older, out-of-date will, it could cause serious legal and financial problems for your estate. Your executor might have to undo everything and start over again, with your estate footing the bill.

11. Revoking Your Will

A will is not a binding contract on you once it is made (unless you have made it part of a contractual agreement, which is most often unwise and should not even be attempted without a lawyer's help). You can revoke or alter your will at any time before your death, usually by writing and signing a new will that meets the legal requirements. As a precaution, you should include language in your will expressly revoking all prior wills and codicils.

A will can also be presumed revoked if the testator destroys it physically, such as by ripping it up or burning it. However, to validly revoke a will, you must destroy it with the actual intent of revoking it. An accidental tearing, burning, or loss of the will is not enough. For example, your will is not revoked merely because you accidentally threw it in the trash.

But an accidental destruction can cause problems. Someone who wants to challenge your will could argue that you actually intended to revoke it. The resulting legal dispute could be costly and could result in your will being declared invalid. If you accidentally damage or lose your will, make a new one immediately to prevent any confusion over whether you did or did not intend to revoke it.

Also keep in mind that revoking a will usually does *not* make an earlier will effective again. Photocopies of a revoked will are not themselves legally binding, but they can nonetheless cause problems, such as someone who would receive property under your will going to court to argue that you actually did not destroy and did not revoke the will, but merely lost the original. Photocopies can be used to reestablish a will that is merely lost, as opposed to one that has been revoked. Sometimes, there may simply be no proof you actually destroyed the will with the intent to revoke it, and the result could be a costly challenge that could eat up the assets in your estate.

If you intend to revoke your will, it is wise to contact anyone holding a copy of your will and ask him or her to send it to you so that you can destroy it at the same time you destroy the original. Of course, you should make a new will as soon as possible. You should also make sure your named executor knows about the new will and where it is located.

12. Making Copies of Your Will

You should make a few copies of your will after you have signed it and had it witnessed and notarized, but be very careful to sign the original only. Never sign and witness a copy, because that makes it the same as the original, which means you have more than one original existing. Suppose you destroy one, but not both, of these originals. The court will not know if you destroyed the original with an intention to revoke both it and the second original. If a signed and witnessed copy is found ripped up, a probate judge might conclude you intended to revoke it by destroying it. This could be used as evidence that the second original was also revoked. At the very least, this situation will create needless confusion that could ultimately require further court proceedings to resolve. It could also result in needless expense to your estate.

13. A Simple Will

Sample 2 shows a simple will written by perhaps the most common type of testator — someone who wants only to leave his estate to his closest family members, is confident his estate will not be taxed, and is not afraid his will might be challenged in court. In fact, because he is leaving his estate to his "natural heirs," it is unlikely anyone would challenge this will.

Let's examine the way this will is written and look at what is included. The following discussion will help you as you think about preparing your own will.

13.1 Opening clause

In the first paragraph, Mr. Jones says that he is signing the document as his last will and testament. This statement simply establishes that he knows he is creating a will and intends it to be honored as such. Paragraph 1 also includes information to help show that Mr. Jones is fully aware of what he is doing and is of "sound and disposing mind" as discussed in section **3.** earlier in this chapter.

Remember that simply saying that you have a "disposing mind" does not necessarily prove it is so. That is why in the second sentence of paragraph 1, Mr. Jones actually names his natural heirs: his wife, children, and grandchildren. Doing so shows

SIMPLE WILL

LAST WILL AND TESTAMENT OF

❧❧ Robert K. Jones, Sr. ❧❧

I, Robert K. Jones, Sr., being of sound and disposing mind, declare this to be my last will and testament. My closest family consists of my wife Helene Jones, our two children Dara Jones Wilson and Robert K. Jones, Jr., both now adults, and three grandchildren. I was born November 14, 1940, and currently am a resident of Orange County, Florida. I revoke all prior wills and codicils I have made.

Executor. I name my wife, Helene Jones, as my executor. If she cannot serve, I name my daughter Dara Jones Wilson as my executor. My executor(s) shall serve without bond; shall have authority to appoint a successor, alternate, or coexecutor; shall exercise the fullest extent of authority allowed by law to an executor; and may administer my estate by any alternative method allowed by law.

Gifts. I give my entire estate to my wife, Helene Jones, but if she fails to survive me by more than 30 days, I give my entire estate to my two children Dara Jones Wilson and Robert K. Jones, Jr., in equal shares, per stirpes to their descendants if either or both fail to survive me by 30 days.

This is the conclusion of my last will and testament.

In witness whereof I have signed this Last Will & Testament in Orange County, in the State of Florida, on the 11th day of May in the Year 2001.

_____

Robert K. Jones, Sr.

The foregoing was signed by Robert K. Jones, Sr., the testator, in our presence and we have signed our names as witnesses in Orange County, Florida, on May 11, 2001.

_____

Jeanette Bassett
5151 W. 17th St.
Orlando FL 32801

_____

Vincent St. Michael
356 Orange Blossom Trail
Orlando FL 32806

_____

Harold T. Evans
47 W. 14th St.
Orlando FL 32804

AFFIDAVIT

STATE OF FLORIDA
COUNTY OF ORANGE

We, Robert K. Jones, Sr., Testator, and the witnesses, Jeanette Bassett, Vincent St. Michael, and Harold T. Evans, whose names are signed to the attached or foregoing instrument, having been sworn, declared to the undersigned notary that the Testator, in the presence of the witnesses, signed or directed another to sign this instrument as the Testator's Last Will & Testament; and that each of the witnesses, in the presence of the Testator and in the presence of each other, signed this Last Will & Testament as a witness.

TESTATOR: _____
Robert K. Jones, Sr.

WITNESS: _____
Printed Name: Jeanette Bassett
Address: 5151 W. 17th St.
Orlando FL 32801

WITNESS: _____
Printed Name: Vincent St. Michael
Address: 356 Orange Blossom Trail
Orlando FL 32806

WITNESS: _____
Printed Name: Harold T. Evans
Address: 47 W. 14th St.
Orlando FL 32804

Subscribed and sworn to before me by Robert K. Jones, Sr., the Testator, and by Jeanette Bassett, Vincent St. Michael, and Harold T. Evans, the Witnesses, on the 11th day of May in the year 2001.

_____
NOTARY PUBLIC SEAL

My Commission Expires _____

that he is well aware of who would receive his property if he died without a will.

Then in the third sentence, Mr. Jones states his birthday and county of residence, providing more evidence that he knows how old he is and thus is of "disposing mind." By naming the county of residence, he also indicates the state laws that would normally govern his will. In most instances, using this language is merely a precaution. Judges tend to resolve doubts about a will in favor of its validity. The issue of whether or not the testator was of "disposing mind" normally will not come up unless someone challenges the will. Still, it is wise to take the precaution and include the information.

Mr. Jones also takes the precaution in paragraph 1 of revoking all prior wills and codicils he has signed. As discussed in section **11.** earlier, this simply makes plain that the document is the most up-to-date will. People include this clause in their wills even if they have no prior wills or codicils.

13.2 Executor clause

The second paragraph of Mr. Jones's will deals with his executor. Like many people, he wants his executor to be the member of his family who also will inherit all or some of his estate. He might not want to do this if he had reason to believe that one or more family members might challenge his will. In that instance, it might be better to have a neutral executor who would not be accused of abusing his or her authority. But it is obvious that Mr. Jones foresees no such problems.

Note that Mr. Jones takes care to name an alternate executor in case his first choice does not qualify. This could be important if, for example, his wife is alive but mentally unfit to serve as executor. In this way, he plans for future contingencies.

Mr. Jones also says his executor will serve without having to post a bond to guarantee faithful performance under the terms of the will. Since Mr. Jones is giving his estate to his executor, the cost of the bond would only diminish the assets left to his family.

Next, Mr. Jones gives his executor the authority to name a successor, alternate, or coexecutor. Such authority may be useful if, for example, the executor believes it would be better for someone else to serve in this role.

Finally, Mr. Jones states his intention that his executor should have the fullest degree of authority available under state law and can use any available alternative method of probating the estate. As discussed in section **4.** earlier in this chapter, giving an executor this kind of authority is common for smaller estates because it gives the executor greater leeway in settling the estate. However, it is also possible to impose restrictions on the executor's authority.

13.3 Gift clause

The third paragraph in the sample will is also typical of wills that want to provide for immediate family. In the sample, Mr. Jones's entire estate goes to his wife if she is still alive *and* if she survives him by more than 30 days. If Mr. Jones's wife is dead or dies within 30 days of his death, his estate goes in equal shares to his two children, subject again to the 30-day clause. (For more information on a 30-day clause, see section **5.3** earlier in this chapter.) Figure 1 shows what would happen to Mr. Jones's estate in that case.

Yet, Mr. Jones does not stop there in planning for unknown future events. He also includes language to say what will happen if one or both of his children die before he does or if they die within 30 days of his death. Note the use of the phrase "per stirpes." Remember that those words, which mean "by the root," determine who will get what portions of Mr. Jones's estate if his named beneficiaries die before he does. By using this language, Mr. Jones is saying that each set of grandchildren is entitled to divide their dead parents' half share. In other words, the estate will be divided in two after Mr. Jones dies. *Then* the grandchildren in each child's family will receive an equal share of their parents' half. Figure 2 shows how the estate would be divided in this case if Mr. Jones's son had only one child and his daughter had two children. As you can see, the estate is divided as though both children were still alive *before* it is redivided among the grandchildren.

FIGURE #1

PER STIRPES DISTRIBUTION TO TWO CHILDREN IF SPOUSE IS ALREADY DECEASED

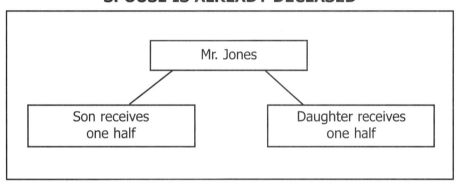

FIGURE #2

PER STIRPES DISTRIBUTION WITH BOTH CHILDREN DECEASED AND THREE SURVIVING GRANDCHILDREN

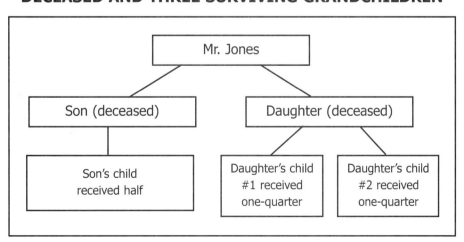

Note that the use of language like "per stirpes" is done only as a precaution. There are ways of achieving different results. One other way is called "per capita." Suppose Mr. Jones's wife and both children are dead and he wants to leave an equal share of his estate *only* to his surviving grandchildren. In other words, he does not intend to leave anything to the offspring of any grandchild who dies before he does. He could do so with the following language:

> *I give my entire estate in equal shares per capita to my grandchildren Robert K. Jones III, Sally Anne Wilson, and Damian Wilson, Jr.*

This language would give an equal portion of the estate only to the named grandchildren still living when Mr. Jones died, assuming they had no children of their own. If one were dead by then without offspring, the other two would each receive one half of the estate. If two were dead without offspring, the only surviving grandchild would receive the entire estate. **Caution:** If all of the grandchildren were dead by then without offspring and no other beneficiaries were named, there would be no one left to inherit under this will. As a result, Mr. Jones's estate would be distributed under the law of intestate succession. If this is not what he wanted, then it would be important to name an alternate beneficiary like another relative, a friend, or a charity, although it would be far better if Mr. Jones updated his will upon the deaths of *anyone* named in his will.

If Mr. Jones wanted his estate to go to a charity if all his grandchildren were dead, he might use the following language:

> *If all of my three grandchildren fail to survive me, I leave my entire estate to the Orlando Area Humane Society whose offices are at 111 Orange Boulevard in Orlando, Florida.*

Here, Mr. Jones not only names the charity but gives its actual business address. This is a wise precaution when leaving all or part of an estate to an organization that may have many branches or local and national chapters. For instance, simply leaving his estate to the humane society would create confusion. Does he mean the national organization or a local, state, or regional branch? The issue might have to be settled in court, which could delay closing the entire estate.

As mentioned earlier, it is far better to revise your will to specifically name each of your beneficiaries and what share they will receive. This is true even if you must revise your will frequently to keep up with the births or deaths of children or grandchildren or other events in your life. Legal phrases like "per stirpes" and "per capita" are merely precautions used in the event that, for whatever reason, you cannot or do not update your will to reflect changing family circumstances. Always keep in mind that "per stirpes" means that your beneficiary's lineal descendants will divide his or her share if that beneficiary dies before you do. "Per capita" means you want property divided equally among only those named beneficiaries who are still alive when you die.

13.4 Concluding clause

The final portion of Mr. Jones's will simply notes that the will is concluded and gives the date and place the will was signed and witnessed. It is useful to note the point at which the will is finished dividing property. This helps prevent the possibility that someone might try to put an additional clause in your will without your knowledge.

Wills also should include a clause that says that you have signed it as your will. This is sometimes called the "testamonium clause." This section should also include the printed names and addresses of the witnesses who sign the document. Printing out names is a good precaution in these days when bad penmanship is commonplace and signatures may be hard to read. Similarly, it is wise to include the current addresses of the witnesses to help identify who signed the will and make it easier to find them if questions arise about the will's validity. If someone challenges the will, for instance, it may be necessary to call the witnesses into court to testify about what they saw. Also note that three witnesses have signed this will. Most states require only two witness signatures, though a few require three. But including an extra signature is a good precaution because it will make things easier if one of the other witnesses cannot be located if needed to verify the will.

13.5 Notarized affidavit

Finally, Mr. Jones has attached to his will a notarized affidavit. As discussed in section **8.** eariler in this chapter, a self-proof affidavit is not a legal necessity, but it does offer a significant advantage of providing further evidence of the will's validity.

14. A More Complex Will

Sample 3 shows an example of a more complex will. In this case, the testator has two minor children, and so she includes a clause to nominate a guardian should her husband predecease her. (See section **5.5** for more information on clauses related to minor children.)

This will also grants specific bequests and shows the language to use. Remember that if you plan to leave particular pieces of property, it is very important to specifically identify them. (See section **5.2** for more information.)

15. Summary of Steps

If you are going to draft your own will, remember the following:

(a) Complete an inventory of your estate.

(b) Make a draft of your will, setting out the names of the people whom you want to receive your property. Also list the specific gifts or percentage of your estate they will receive. Be sure that all beneficiaries and the nature of the gifts to them are clearly identified.

(c) Name your executor and any alternative executor.

(d) Type the document, but do not sign it. If you must write the document by hand, make sure it is easily readable.

(e) Arrange to meet with your witnesses at the office of a notary public where you can sign the document and have it witnessed all in the presence of each other. Don't forget to initial or sign the bottom of each page of the will.

(f) Place your valid will and your property inventory in a safe, fireproof place and tell your executor where it is. Remember that if you make copies of your will, sign the original only.

(g) Review your will regularly and update it if necessary. Keep in mind that laws change constantly, so you should make sure you have the most recent edition of this book.

WILL NOMINATING A GUARDIAN

Last Will & Testament of

⚜ Eileen Carr Strait ⚜

I, Eileen Carr Strait, being of sound and disposing mind, declare this to be my last will and testament. My closest family consists of my husband Jacob Harold Strait, our two minor children Tammi Lynn Strait and Jacob Carr Strait. I was born January 2, 1961, and currently am a resident of Dade County, Florida. I revoke all prior wills and codicils I have made.

Executor. I name my husband Jacob Harold Strait as my executor. If he cannot serve, I name my sister Helen Carr Burrell as my executor. My executor shall serve without bond; shall have authority to appoint a successor, alternate, or coexecutor; shall exercise the fullest extent of authority allowed by law to an executor; and may administer my estate by any alternative method allowed by law.

Gifts. Subject to the exceptions below, I give my entire estate to my husband Jacob Harold Strait. However, if my husband Jacob Harold Strait fails to survive me by more than 30 days, I give my entire estate to my children Tammi Lynn Strait and Jacob Carr Strait in equal shares, subject to the exceptions below.

Exceptions. Notwithstanding the above gifts, I give my wedding ring, which is an heirloom used by my grandmother as her wedding ring, to my sister Helen Carr Burrell. I further give my 2000 model Cadillac Sedan DeVille, vehicle identification number #555555, to my sister Helen Carr Burrell.

Nomination of Guardian. If my husband, Jacob Harold Strait, predeceases me, or if we both die simultaneously, I nominate my sister Helen Carr Burrell as the guardian of my minor children Tammi Lynn Strait and Jacob Carr Strait because of the love and affection Helen Carr Burrell has shown them from the time of their births and because they regard her as a second mother.

This is the conclusion of my last will and testament.

In witness whereof I have signed this Last Will & Testament in Dade County, in the State of Florida, on the 7th day of January in the Year 2001.

_____

Eileen Carr Strait

The foregoing was signed by Eileen Carr Strait, the testator, in our presence and we have signed our names as witnesses in Orange County, Florida, on January 7, 2001.

_____

John Thoms
5151 W. 17th St.
Miami FL 33311

Denise Johnston
356 S. Brickell Avenue
Miami FL 33311

Wayne Dewey Prescott
47 Morningside Lane
Coconut Grove FL 33311

AFFIDAVIT

STATE OF FLORIDA
COUNTY OF MIAMI-DADE

We, Eileen Carr Strait, Testator, and the witnesses, John Thoms, Denise Johnston, and Wayne Dewey Prescott, whose names are signed to the attached or foregoing instrument, having been sworn, declared to the undersigned notary that the Testator, in the presence of the witnesses, signed or directed another to sign this instrument as the Testator's Last Will & Testament; and that each of the witnesses, in the presence of the Testator and in the presence of each other, signed this Last Will & Testament as a witness.

TESTATOR: _____
          Eileen Carr Strait

WITNESS: _____
          Printed Name: John Thoms
          Address: 5151 W. 17th St.
            Miami FL 33311

WITNESS: _____
          Printed Name: Denise Johnston
          Address: 356 S. Brickell Avenue
            Miami FL 33311

WITNESS: _____
          Printed Name: Wayne Dewey Prescott
          Address: 47 Morningside Lane
            Coconut Grove FL 33311

Subscribed and sworn to before me by Eileen Carr Strait, the Testator, and by John Thoms, Denise Johnston, and Wayne Dewey Prescott, the Witnesses, on the 7th day of January in the year 2001.

_____

NOTARY PUBLIC SEAL

My Commission Expires _____

Part 3
Beyond the Will:
Other Estate Planning Tools

8
Living Wills and Powers of Attorney

In addition to writing a will, anyone involved in estate planning should consider two other kinds of legal documents:

(a) Living wills (also called advance directives)

(b) Powers of attorney

Unlike a will, these documents take effect while you are still alive. They are designed to help those around you deal with problems that may arise if you become so ill that you are unable to make decisions for yourself. As a result, they can be very important in estate planning.

Note: The law on this subject is changing rapidly and varies tremendously from state to state. A new trend is to combine both kinds of documents — the living will and the power of attorney — into a single all-purpose document governing health-care decision making. But some states still use separate forms.

At the end of this chapter you will find sample forms suggested by the laws of many states, divided into these three categories:

(a) States with separate living-will forms

(b) States with separate power-of-attorney forms

(c) States that combine the two in some way

Not all states have laws suggesting the types of forms to use, and some states may have one type of form but not another. Because of the rapid changes in the laws concerning living wills (advance directives) and powers of attorney, you should *always* check with your state bar association (see Appendix) to obtain the most recently adopted forms in your state.

1. Living Will

There has been much talk in the last two decades about the "right to die," and the courts have had to determine many cases regarding whether or not a patient can refuse life-prolonging medical care in the final stages of life. As a result, most states now recognize a "right to die" for people who are terminally ill (including those who can no longer communicate) and cannot continue to survive without constant medical treatment.

The decision to stop medical treatment is often based on a living will, also called an advance directive, which a person signs before he or she reaches the final stages of an illness. In fact, you can create and sign a living will even before you become sick. A living will simply says how you feel about medical care that would artificially prolong your life. It instructs your medical-care providers and family to withdraw artificial life support at a certain point, although it can also be used to say that you actually *want* your life prolonged by artificial means. Most people, however, do not use it to prolong dying because they feel this would be undignified and could require that a great deal of money be spent for no good purpose.

The exact forms for living wills or advance directives differ widely from state to state and from time to time. For this reason, no single form will work in all of the states. However, there are resources that will make advance directive forms available to you at little or no cost. Hospitals usually have blank copies of the form used in your state. You also may be able to find them from your local or state bar association, local public library, and government programs for the elderly. The Appendix shows a list of addresses of state bar associations. You can contact these offices to ask for standard forms for your state. Sample forms contained in the laws of many states are also included at the end of this chapter.

2. Power of Attorney

Many people understand that an "attorney at law" is someone licensed to practice law in a particular state. However, many people do not know that there is something else called an "attorney in fact." Attorneys in fact are simply people you appoint to make decisions on your behalf. They act as your substitute decision-maker and do not need to be actual attorneys at law. You designate someone as your attorney in fact in a legal document called a power of attorney. Always remember, however, that a power of attorney does not authorize someone to act as your lawyer. It authorizes someone only to be your substitute decision-maker. No one but a licensed attorney can practice law in your state.

Powers of attorney have long been used in business transactions in which one person (called a "principal") gives a representative (the attorney in fact) power to make legally binding decisions on her or his behalf. At all times the principal can revoke the power of attorney, and the power also automatically ends if the principal becomes incapacitated or dies. This kind of substitute decision-making goes far back into legal history.

The major drawback to a power of attorney is that it automatically ceases to exist if the principal dies or loses mental faculties. Many disputes have arisen over whether principals, in fact, were mentally sound and, if not, when the loss of mental faculties occurred. At times, very important business decisions hinged on determining at exactly what moment the principal lost soundness of mind. Expensive lawsuits often resulted.

This problem led to reforms. In recent years, the law on powers of attorney has been expanded to deal with other situations. There have been two major developments:

(a) The durable power of attorney

(b) The health-care power of attorney

2.1 Durable power of attorney

A durable power of attorney is one that continues to exist even if the principal becomes incapacitated. It was developed to help people name a representative to take care of their everyday business and financial affairs if they were unable to do so themselves. Usually, it is necessary to fill out a special form to enforce a durable power of attorney. As with living wills, these forms vary widely from state to state.

You should talk to a lawyer before you sign any kind of durable power of attorney. In some states, granting these powers can lead to problems. Sometimes the power you grant to your attorney in fact can be used immediately, whether or not you are sick. If you make a poor choice for your attorney-in-fact, that person could sell your property or handle your assets in ways you did not intend. This is a serious problem that has led some states to develop alternative procedures. One involves designating a "preneed guardian" who will be able to step in and handle your affairs under court supervision if you are unable to do so. Because the laws on the subject vary so much from state to state, you need to get the advice of a lawyer licensed in your state to help you in this area.

2.2 Health-care power of attorney

Some states also have tried other ways to reduce the problems that can be caused by durable powers of attorney. One is the health-care power of attorney, also called a "health-care surrogacy" or a "health-care proxy." This document lets you name

another person to make decisions on your behalf if you cannot —
but *solely* on questions concerning the health care you will receive. Health-care "substitutes" typically cannot make business
decisions for you, for instance, but they can tell a doctor whether
or not to give you a particular form of treatment.

These forms, wherever adopted, have made it much easier for
Americans to name substitute decision-makers easily and at little
expense. As a general rule, your health-care substitute is sup-
posed to honor your wishes as you have expressed them. Forms
in some states even include spaces for you to state your wishes
about certain kinds of health-care decisions or medical procedures.

Nevertheless, health-care substitutes should be chosen with
care, as they literally can make life-or-death decisions for you.
Once again, the law on health-care substitutes varies widely from
state to state; if there is a form available for your state, you
should be able to locate it from the same sources that will provide
you with blank living wills. (See section **1.** earlier in this chapter and
the Appendix.)

Many states have laws suggesting the form for choosing a
health-care substitute. Samples from a number of states are located at the end of this chapter.

Sample Forms:

Living Wills

The sample forms following are suggested by the laws of those states that allow living wills. See also the sections following this one for power of attorney forms and for forms that combine living wills and powers of attorney in some way.

Always remember that the laws concerning living wills are changing, and you must check that you have the most recent form before you fill one out.

Included in this section are forms for the following states:

- Arizona
- Colorado
- Connecticut
- District of Columbia
- Florida
- Georgia
- Illinois

- Louisiana
- North Carolina
- Tennessee
- Texas
- Utah
- Washington

111

Arizona Living Will

Some general statements concerning your health-care options are outlined below. If you agree with one of the statements, you should initial that statement. Read all of these statements carefully before you initial your selection. You can also write your own statement concerning life-sustaining treatment and other matters relating to your health care. You may initial any combination of paragraphs 1, 2, 3, and 4, but if you initial paragraph 5, the others should not be initialed.

_____ 1. If I have a terminal condition, I do not want my life to be prolonged and I do not want life-sustaining treatment, beyond comfort care, that would serve only to artificially delay the moment of my death.

_____ 2. If I am in a terminal condition, or an irreversible coma, or a persistent vegetative state that my doctors reasonably feel to be irreversible or incurable, I do want the medical treatment necessary to provide care that would keep me comfortable, but I do not want the following:

        _____ (a) Cardiopulmonary resuscitation; for example, the use of drugs, electric shock, and artificial breathing

        _____ (b) Artificially administered food and fluids

        _____ (c) To be taken to a hospital if at all avoidable

_____ 3. Notwithstanding my other directions, if I am known to be pregnant, I do not want life-sustaining treatment withheld or withdrawn if it is possible that the embryo/fetus will develop to the point of live birth with the continued application of life-sustaining treatment.

_____ 4. Notwithstanding my other directions I do want the use of all medical care necessary to treat my condition until my doctors reasonably conclude that my condition is terminal or is irreversible and incurable or I am in a persistent vegetative state.

_____ 5. I want my life to be prolonged to the greatest extent possible.

Other or Additional Statements of Desires

I have_____ I have not_____ attached additional special provisions or limitations to this document to be honored in the absence of my being able to give health-care directions.

Dated at _____, Arizona, this _____ day of _____, 20_____.

_____ Name and Address

_____ Name and Address

STATE OF ARIZONA)

) ss.

County of _____)

SUBSCRIBED and sworn to before me by _____,
the declarant, and _____ and _____, witnesses, as the voluntary act
and deed of the declarant this_____ day of _____, 20_____.

My commission expires:_____

Colorado Declaration as to Medical or Surgical Treatment

I, _____ (name of declarant), being of sound mind and at least 18 years of age, direct that my life shall not be artificially prolonged under the circumstances set forth below and hereby declare that:

1. If at any time my attending physician and one other qualified physician certify in writing that:

a. I have an injury, disease, or illness which is not curable or reversible and which, in their judgment, is a terminal condition, and

b. For a period of seven consecutive days or more, I have been unconscious, comatose, or otherwise incompetent so as to be unable to make or communicate responsible decisions concerning my person, then

I direct that, in accordance with Colorado law, life-sustaining procedures shall be withdrawn and withheld pursuant to the terms of this declaration, it being understood that life-sustaining procedures shall not include any medical procedure or intervention for nourishment considered necessary by the attending physician to provide comfort or alleviate pain. However, I may specifically direct, in accordance with Colorado law, that artificial nourishment be withdrawn or withheld pursuant to the terms of this declaration.

2. In the event that the only procedure I am being provided is artificial nourishment, I direct that one of the following actions be taken:

_____ (initials of declarant) a. Artificial nourishment shall not be continued when it is the only procedure being provided; or

_____ (initials of declarant) b. Artificial nourishment shall be continued for _____ days when it is the only procedure being provided; or

_____ (initials of declarant) c. Artificial nourishment shall be continued when it is the only procedure being provided.

3. I execute this declaration, as my free and voluntary act, this _____ day of

_____ , 20 _____.

By _____ Declarant

The foregoing instrument was signed and declared by _____ to be his declaration, in the presence of us, who, in his or her presence, in the presence of each other, and at his or her request, have signed our names below as witnesses, and we declare that, at the time of the execution of this instrument, the declarant, according to our best knowledge and belief, was of sound mind and under no constraint or undue influence.

Dated at _____, Colorado, this _____ day of _____, 20_____.

_____ Name and Address

_____ Name and Address

STATE OF COLORADO)

) ss.

County of _____)

SUBSCRIBED and sworn to before me by _____, the declarant, and _____ and _____, witnesses, as the voluntary act and deed of the declarant this _____ day of _____, 20 _____.

My commission expires: _____

Connecticut Document Concerning Withholding or Withdrawal of Life Support Systems

If the time comes when I am incapacitated to the point when I can no longer actively take part in decisions for my own life, and am unable to direct my physician as to my own medical care, I wish this statement to stand as a testament of my wishes.

"I, _____ (Name), request that, if my condition is deemed terminal or if it is determined that I will be permanently unconscious, I be allowed to die and not be kept alive through life-support systems. By terminal condition, I mean that I have an incurable or irreversible medical condition which, without the administration of life-support systems, will, in the opinion of my attending physician, result in death within a relatively short time. By permanently unconscious I mean that I am in a permanent coma or persistent vegetative state which is an irreversible condition in which I am at no time aware of myself or the environment and show no behavioral response to the environment. The life-support systems which I do not want include, but are not limited to:

- Artificial respiration
- Cardiopulmonary resuscitation
- Artificial means of providing nutrition and hydration

(Cross out and initial life-support systems you want administered.)

I do not intend any direct taking of my life, but only that my dying not be unreasonably prolonged."

Other specific requests:

"This request is made, after careful reflection, while I am of sound mind."

_____ (Signature)

_____ (Date)

This document was signed in our presence, by the above-named,

_____ (Name),

who appeared to be 18 years of age or older, of sound mind and able to understand the nature and consequences of health-care decisions at the time the document was signed.

_____ (Witness)

_____ (Address)

_____ (Witness)

_____ (Address)

District of Columbia Declaration

Declaration made this_____ day of _____ (month, year).

I,_____, being of sound mind, willfully and voluntarily make known my desires that my dying shall not be artificially prolonged under the circumstances set forth below, do declare:

If at any time I should have an incurable injury, disease, or illness certified to be a terminal condition by two physicians who have personally examined me, one of whom shall be my attending physician, and the physicians have determined that my death will occur whether or not life-sustaining procedures are utilized and where the application of life-sustaining procedures would serve only to artificially prolong the dying process, I direct that such procedures be withheld or withdrawn, and that I be permitted to die naturally with only the administration of medication or the performance of any medical procedure deemed necessary to provide me with comfort care or to alleviate pain.

In the absence of my ability to give directions regarding the use of such life-sustaining procedures, it is my intention that this declaration shall be honored by my family and physician(s) as the final expression of my legal right to refuse medical or surgical treatment and accept the consequences from such refusal.

I understand the full import of this declaration and I am emotionally and mentally competent to make this declaration.

Signed _____

Address_____

I believe the declarant to be of sound mind. I did not sign the declarant's signature above for or at the direction of the declarant. I am at least 18 years of age and am not related to the declarant by blood or marriage, entitled to any portion of the estate of the declarant according to the laws of intestate succession of the District of Columbia or under any will of the declarant or codicil thereto, or directly financially responsible for declarant's medical care. I am not the declarant's attending physician, an employee of the attending physician, or an employee of the health facility in which the declarant is a patient.

Signed _____

Address_____

Florida Living Will

Declaration made this _____ day of _____, _____

I, _____,

willfully and voluntarily make known my desire that my dying not be artificially prolonged under the circumstances set forth below, and I do hereby declare that, if at any time
I am incapacitated and

_____ (initial) I have a terminal condition,

or_____ (initial) I have an end-stage condition,

or_____ (initial) I am in a persistent vegetative state,

and if my attending or treating physician and another consulting physician have determined that there is no reasonable medical probability of my recovery from such condition,
I direct that life-prolonging procedures be withheld or withdrawn when the application of
such procedures would serve only to prolong artificially the process of dying, and that I be
permitted to die naturally with only the administration of medication or the performance
of any medical procedure deemed necessary to provide me with comfort care or to alleviate pain.

It is my intention that this declaration be honored by my family and physician as the
final expression of my legal right to refuse medical or surgical treatment and to accept the
consequences for such refusal.

In the event that I have been determined to be unable to provide express and informed
consent regarding the withholding, withdrawal, or continuation of life-prolonging procedures, I wish to designate, as my surrogate to carry out the provisions of this declaration:

Name:_____

Address:_____

_____Zip Code:_____

Phone: _____

I understand the full import of this declaration, and I am emotionally and mentally competent to make this declaration.

Additional Instructions (optional):

_____

_____

Signed: _____

Witness: _____

Address:_____

Phone: _____

Witness: _____

Address:_____

Phone: _____

Georgia Living Will

Living will made this _____ day of_____ (month, year).

I, _____, being of sound mind, willfully and voluntarily make known my desire that my life shall not be prolonged under the circumstances set forth below and do declare:

1. If at any time I should (check each option desired):

   (___) have a terminal condition,

   (___) become in a coma with no reasonable expectation of regaining consciousness, or

   (___) become in a persistent vegetative state with no reasonable expectation of regaining significant cognitive function, as defined in and established in accordance with the procedures set forth in paragraphs (2), (9), and (13) of Code Section 31-32-2 of the Official Code of Georgia Annotated, I direct that the application of life-sustaining procedures to my body (check the option desired):

   (___) including nourishment and hydration,

   (___) including nourishment but not hydration, or

   (___) excluding nourishment and hydration,

   be withheld or withdrawn and that I be permitted to die;

2. In the absence of my ability to give directions regarding the use of such life-sustaining procedures, it is my intention that this living will shall be honored by my family and physician(s) as the final expression of my legal right to refuse medical or surgical treatment and accept the consequences from such refusal;

3. I understand that I may revoke this living will at any time;

4. I understand the full import of this living will, and I am at least 18 years of age and am emotionally and mentally competent to make this living will; and

5. If I am a female and I have been diagnosed as pregnant, this living will shall have no force and effect unless the fetus is not viable and I indicate by initialing after this sentence that I want this living will to be carried out. (Initial) _____

Signed _____

_____ (City), _____ (County), and _____ (State of Residence).

I hereby witness this living will and attest that:

(1) The declarant is personally known to me and I believe the declarant to be at least 18 years of age and of sound mind;

(2) I am at least 18 years of age;

(3) To the best of my knowledge, at the time of the execution of this living will, I:

(A) Am not related to the declarant by blood or marriage;

(B) Would not be entitled to any portion of the declarant's estate by any will or by operation of law under the rules of descent and distribution of this state;

(C) Am not the attending physician of the declarant or an employee of the attending physician or an employee of the hospital or skilled nursing facility in which declarant is a patient;

(D) Am not directly financially responsible for the declarant's medical care; and

(E) Have no present claim against any portion of the estate of the declarant;

(4) Declarant has signed this document in my presence as above instructed, on the date above first shown.

Witness _____

Address_____

Witness _____

Address_____

Additional witness required when living will is signed in a hospital or skilled nursing facility:

I hereby witness this living will and attest that I believe the declarant to be of sound mind and to have made this living will willingly and voluntarily.

Witness _____

Medical director of skilled nursing facility or staff physician not participating in care of the patient or chief of the hospital medical staff or staff physician or hospital designee not participating in care of the patient.

Illinois Declaration

This declaration is made this_____ day of _____ (month, year). I,_____, being of sound mind, willfully and voluntarily make known my desires that my moment of death shall not be artificially postponed.

If at any time I should have an incurable and irreversible injury, disease, or illness judged to be a terminal condition by my attending physician who has personally examined me and has determined that my death is imminent except for death-delaying procedures, I direct that such procedures which would only prolong the dying process be withheld or withdrawn, and that I be permitted to die naturally with only the administration of medication, sustenance, or the performance of any medical procedure deemed necessary by my attending physician to provide me with comfort care.

In the absence of my ability to give directions regarding the use of such death-delaying procedures, it is my intention that this declaration shall be honored by my family and physician as the final expression of my legal right to refuse medical or surgical treatment and accept the consequences from such refusal.

Signed_____

City, County and State of Residence_____

The declarant is personally known to me, and I believe him or her to be of sound mind. I saw the declarant sign the declaration in my presence (or the declarant acknowledged in my presence that he or she had signed the declaration) and I signed the declaration as a witness in the presence of the declarant. I did not sign the declarant's signature above for or at the direction of the declarant. At the date of this instrument, I am not entitled to any portion of the estate of the declarant according to the laws of intestate succession or, to the best of my knowledge and belief, under any will of declarant or other instrument taking effect at declarant's death, or directly financially responsible for declarant's medical care.

Witness _____

Witness _____

Louisiana Declaration

This declaration is made this _____ day of _____ (month, year). I,_____, being of sound mind, willfully and voluntarily make known my desire that my dying shall not be artificially prolonged under the circumstances set forth below and do hereby declare:

If at any time I should have an incurable injury, disease or illness, or be in a continual profound comatose state with no reasonable chance of recovery, certified to be a terminal and irreversible condition by two physicians who have personally examined me, one of whom shall be my attending physician, and the physicians have determined that my death will occur whether or not life-sustaining procedures are utilized and where the application of life-sustaining procedure would serve only to prolong artificially the dying process, I direct that such procedures be withheld or withdrawn and that I be permitted to die naturally with only the administration of medication or the performance of any medical procedure deemed necessary to provide me with comfort care.

In the absence of my ability to give directions regarding the use of such life-sustaining procedures, it is my intention that this declaration shall be honored by my family and physician(s) as the final expression of my legal right to refuse medical or surgical treatment and accept the consequences from such refusal.

I understand the full import of this declaration and I am emotionally and mentally competent to make this declaration.

Signed _____

City, Parish and State of Residence _____

The declarant has been personally known to me and I believe him or her to be of sound mind.

Witness _____

Witness _____

North Carolina Declaration of Desire for a Natural Death

I, _____, being of sound mind, desire that, as specified below, my life not be prolonged by extraordinary means or by artificial nutrition or hydration if my condition is determined to be terminal and incurable or if I am diagnosed as being in a persistent vegetative state. I am aware and understand that this writing authorizes a physician to withhold or discontinue extraordinary means or artificial nutrition or hydration, in accordance with my specifications set forth below:

(Initial any of the following, as desired):

_____ If my condition is determined to be terminal and incurable, I authorize the following:

       _____ My physician may withhold or discontinue extraordinary means only.

_____ In addition to withholding or discontinuing extraordinary means if such means are necessary, my physician may withhold or discontinue either artificial nutrition or hydration, or both.

_____ If my physician determines that I am in a persistent vegetative state, I authorize the following:

       _____ My physician may withhold or discontinue extraordinary means only.

_____ In addition to withholding or discontinuing extraordinary means if such means are necessary, my physician may withhold or discontinue either artificial nutrition or hydration, or both.

This the _____ day of _____, _____.

Signature _____

I hereby state that the declarant, _____ being of sound mind signed the above declaration in my presence and that I am not related to the declarant by blood or marriage and that I do not know or have a reasonable expectation that I would be entitled to any portion of the estate of the declarant under any existing will or codicil of the declarant or as an heir under the Intestate Succession Act if the declarant died on this date without a will. I also state that I am not the declarant's attending physician or an employee of the declarant's attending physician, or an employee of a health facility in which the declarant is a patient or an employee of a nursing home or any group-care home where the declarant resides. I further state that I do not now have any claim against the declarant.

Witness _____

Witness _____

The clerk or the assistant clerk, or a notary public may, upon proper proof, certify the declaration as follows:

Certificate

I, _____, Clerk (Assistant Clerk) of Superior Court or Notary Public (circle one as appropriate) for _____ County hereby certify that_____, the declarant, appeared before me and swore to me and to the witnesses in my presence that this instrument is his or her Declaration Of A Desire For A Natural Death, and that he or she had willingly and voluntarily made and executed it as his or her free act and deed for the purposes expressed in it.

I further certify that _____ and _____, witnesses, appeared before me and swore that they witnessed_____, declarant, sign the attached declaration, believing him or her to be of sound mind; and also swore that at the time they witnessed the declaration (i) they were not related within the third degree to the declarant or to the declarant's spouse, and (ii) they did not know or have a reasonable expectation that they would be entitled to any portion of the estate of the declarant upon the declarant's death under any will of the declarant or codicil thereto then existing or under the Intestate Succession Act as it provides at that time, and (iii) they were not a physician attending the declarant or an employee of an attending physician or an employee of a health facility in which the declarant was a patient or an employee of a nursing home or any group-care home in which the declarant resided, and (iv) they did not have a claim against the declarant. I further certify that I am satisfied as to the genuineness and due execution of the declaration.

This the _____day of _____,_____.

Clerk (Assistant Clerk) of Superior Court or Notary Public (circle one as appropriate) for the County of _____.

Tennessee Living Will

I, _____, willfully and voluntarily make known my desire that my dying shall not be artificially prolonged under the circumstances set forth below, and do hereby declare:

If at any time I should have a terminal condition and my attending physician has determined there is no reasonable medical expectation of recovery and which, as a medical probability, will result in my death, regardless of the use or discontinuance of medical treatment implemented for the purpose of sustaining life, or the life process, I direct that medical care be withheld or withdrawn, and that I be permitted to die naturally with only the administration of medications or the performance of any medical procedure deemed necessary to provide me with comfortable care or to alleviate pain.

ARTIFICIALLY PROVIDED NOURISHMENT AND FLUIDS:

By checking the appropriate line below, I specifically:

_____ Authorize the withholding or withdrawal of artificially provided food, water, or other nourishment or fluids.

_____ DO NOT authorize the withholding or withdrawal of artificially provided food, water, or other nourishment or fluids.

ORGAN DONOR CERTIFICATION:

Notwithstanding my previous declaration relative to the withholding or withdrawal of life-prolonging procedures, if as indicated below I have expressed my desire to donate my organs and/or tissues for transplantation, or any of them as specifically designated herein, I do direct my attending physician, if I have been determined dead according to Tennessee Code Annotated, § 68-3-501(b), to maintain me on artificial support systems only for the period of time required to maintain the viability of and to remove such organs and/or tissues.

By checking the appropriate line below, I specifically:

_____ Desire to donate my organs and/or tissues for transplantation.

_____ Desire to donate my _____.

(Insert specific organs and/or tissues for transplantation)

_____ DO NOT desire to donate my organs or tissues for transplantation.

In the absence of my ability to give directions regarding my medical care, it is my intention that this declaration shall be honored by my family and physician as the final expression of my legal right to refuse medical care and accept the consequences of such refusal.

The definitions of terms used herein shall be as set forth in the Tennessee Right to Natural Death Act, Tennessee Code Annotated, § 32-11-103.

I understand the full import of this declaration, and I am emotionally and mentally competent to make this declaration.

In acknowledgment whereof, I do hereinafter affix my signature on this the _____ day of _____, 20 _____.

_____
Declarant

We, the subscribing witnesses hereto, are personally acquainted with and subscribe our names hereto at the request of the declarant, an adult, whom we believe to be of sound mind, fully aware of the action taken herein and its possible consequence.

We, the undersigned witnesses, further declare that we are not related to the declarant by blood or marriage; that we are not entitled to any portion of the estate of the declarant upon the declarant's decease under any will or codicil thereto presently existing or by operation of law then existing; that we are not the attending physician, an employee of the attending physician or a health facility in which the declarant is a patient; and that we are not persons who, at the present time, have a claim against any portion of the estate of the declarant upon the declarant's death.

_____
Witness

_____
Witness

STATE OF TENNESSEE
COUNTY OF

Subscribed, sworn to and acknowledged before me by _____, the declarant, and subscribed and sworn to before me by_____ and _____, witnesses, this _____day of _____, 20 _____.

_____
Notary Public

My Commission Expires:

_____

Texas Directive to Physicians & Family or Surrogates

INSTRUCTIONS FOR COMPLETING THIS DOCUMENT:

This is an important legal document known as an Advance Directive. It is designed to help you communicate your wishes about medical treatment at some time in the future when you are unable to make your wishes known because of illness or injury. These wishes are usually based on personal values. In particular, you may want to consider what burdens or hardships of treatment you would be willing to accept for a particular amount of benefit obtained if you were seriously ill.

You are encouraged to discuss your values and wishes with your family or chosen spokesperson, as well as your physician. Your physician, other health care provider, or medical institution may provide you with various resources to assist you in completing your advance directive. Brief definitions are listed below and may aid you in your discussions and advance planning. Initial the treatment choices that best reflect your personal preferences. Provide a copy of your directive to your physician, usual hospital, and family or spokesperson. Consider a periodic review of this document. By periodic review, you can best assure that the directive reflects your preferences.

In addition to this advance directive, Texas law provides for two other types of directives that can be important during a serious illness. These are the Medical Power of Attorney and the Out-of-Hospital Do-Not-Resuscitate Order. You may wish to discuss these with your physician, family, hospital representative, or other advisers. You may also wish to complete a directive related to the donation of organs and tissues.

DIRECTIVE

I, _____, recognize that the best health care is based upon a partnership of trust and communication with my physician. My physician and I will make health-care decisions together as long as I am of sound mind and able to make my wishes known. If there comes a time that I am unable to make medical decisions about myself because of illness or injury, I direct that the following treatment preferences be honored:

If, in the judgment of my physician, I am suffering with a terminal condition from which I am expected to die within six months, even with available life-sustaining treatment provided in accordance with prevailing standards of medical care:

_____ I request that all treatments other than those needed to keep me comfortable be discontinued or withheld and my physician allow me to die as gently as possible; OR

_____ I request that I be kept alive in this terminal condition using available life-sustaining treatment. (THIS SELECTION DOES NOT APPLY TO HOSPICE CARE.)

If, in the judgment of my physician, I am suffering with an irreversible condition so that I cannot care for myself or make decisions for myself and am expected to die without life-sustaining treatment provided in accordance with prevailing standards of care:

_____ I request that all treatments other than those needed to keep me comfortable be discontinued or withheld and my physician allow me to die as gently as possible; OR

_____ I request that I be kept alive in this irreversible condition using available life-sustaining treatment. (THIS SELECTION DOES NOT APPLY TO HOSPICE CARE.)

Additional requests: (After discussion with your physician, you may wish to consider listing particular treatments in this space that you do or do not want in specific circumstances, such as artificial nutrition and fluids, intravenous antibiotics, etc. Be sure to state whether you do or do not want the particular treatment.)

_____

_____

_____

After signing this directive, if my representative or I elect hospice care, I understand and agree that only those treatments needed to keep me comfortable would be provided and I would not be given available life-sustaining treatments.

If I do not have a Medical Power of Attorney, and I am unable to make my wishes known, I designate the following person(s) to make treatment decisions with my physician compatible with my personal values:

1._____

2._____

(If a Medical Power of Attorney has been executed, then an agent already has been named and you should not list additional names in this document.)

If the above persons are not available, or if I have not designated a spokesperson, I understand that a spokesperson will be chosen for me following standards specified in the laws of Texas. If, in the judgment of my physician, my death is imminent within minutes to hours, even with the use of all available medical treatment provided within the prevailing standard of care, I acknowledge that all treatments may be withheld or removed except those needed to maintain my comfort. I understand that under Texas law this directive has no effect if I have been diagnosed as pregnant. This directive will remain in effect until I revoke it. No other person may do so.

Signed _____Date _____

City, County, State of Residence _____

Two competent adult witnesses must sign below, acknowledging the signature of the declarant. The witness designated as Witness 1 may not be a person designated to make a treatment decision for the patient and may not be related to the patient by blood or marriage. This witness may not be entitled to any part of the estate and may not have a claim against the estate of the patient. This witness may not be the attending physician or an employee of the attending physician. If this witness is an employee of a health-care facility in which the patient is being cared for, this witness may not be involved in providing direct patient care to the patient. This witness may not be an officer, director, partner, or business office employee of a health-care facility in which the patient is being cared for or of any parent organization of the health-care facility.

Witness 1 _____

Witness 2_____

DEFINITIONS:

"Artificial nutrition and hydration" means the provision of nutrients or fluids by a tube inserted in a vein, under the skin in the subcutaneous tissues, or in the stomach (gastrointestinal tract).

"Irreversible condition" means a condition, injury, or illness:

(1) that may be treated, but is never cured or eliminated;

(2) that leaves a person unable to care for or make decisions for the person's own self; and

(3) that, without life-sustaining treatment provided in accordance with the prevailing standard of medical care, is fatal.

Explanation: Many serious illnesses such as cancer, failure of major organs (kidney, heart, liver, or lung), and serious brain disease such as Alzheimer's dementia may be considered irreversible early on. There is no cure, but the patient may be kept alive for prolonged periods of time if the patient receives life-sustaining treatments. Late in the course of the same illness, the disease may be considered terminal when, even with treatment, the patient is expected to die. You may wish to consider which burdens of treatment you would be willing to accept in an effort to achieve a particular outcome. This is a very personal decision that you may wish to discuss with your physician, family, or other important persons in your life.

"Life-sustaining treatment" means treatment that, based on reasonable medical judgment, sustains the life of a patient and without which the patient will die. The term includes both life-sustaining medications and artificial life support such as mechanical breathing machines, kidney dialysis treatment, and artificial hydration and nutrition. The term does not include the administration of pain management medication, the performance of a medical procedure necessary to provide comfort care, or any other medical care provided to alleviate a patient's pain.

"Terminal condition" means an incurable condition caused by injury, disease, or illness that according to reasonable medical judgment will produce death within six months, even with available life-sustaining treatment provided in accordance with the prevailing standard of medical care.

Explanation: Many serious illnesses may be considered irreversible early in the course of the illness, but they may not be considered terminal until the disease is fairly advanced. In thinking about terminal illness and its treatment, you again may wish to consider the relative benefits and burdens of treatment and discuss your wishes with your physician, family, or other important persons in your life.

Utah Directive to Physicians & Providers of Medical Services

(Pursuant to Section 75-2-1104, UCA)

This directive is made this _____ day of _____, _____.

1. I, _____, being of sound mind, willfully and voluntarily make known my desire that my life not be artificially prolonged by life-sustaining procedures except as I may otherwise provide in this directive.

2. I declare that if at any time I should have an injury, disease, or illness, which is certified in writing to be a terminal condition or persistent vegetative state by two physicians who have personally examined me, and in the opinion of those physicians the application of life-sustaining procedures would serve only to unnaturally prolong the moment of my death and to unnaturally postpone or prolong the dying process, I direct that these procedures be withheld or withdrawn and my death be permitted to occur naturally.

3. I expressly intend this directive to be a final expression of my legal right to refuse medical or surgical treatment and to accept the consequences from this refusal which shall remain in effect notwithstanding my future inability to give current medical directions to treating physicians and other providers of medical service.

4. I understand that the term "life-sustaining procedure" includes artificial nutrition and hydration and any other procedures that I specify below to be considered life-sustaining but does not include the administration of medication or the performance of any medical procedure which is intended to provide comfort care or to alleviate pain:

_____

5. I reserve the right to give current medical directions to physicians and other providers of medical services so long as I am able, even though these directions may conflict with the above-written directive that life-sustaining procedures be withheld or withdrawn.

6. I understand the full import of this directive and declare that I am emotionally and mentally competent to make this directive.

_____
Declarant's signature

_____
City, County, and State of Residence

We witnesses certify that each of us is 18 years of age or older and each personally witnessed the declarant sign or direct the signing of this directive; that we are acquainted with the declarant and believe him to be of sound mind; that the declarant's desires are as expressed above; that neither of us is a person who signed the above directive on behalf of the declarant; that we are not related to the declarant by blood or marriage nor are we entitled to any portion of declarant's estate according to the laws of intestate succession of this state or under any will or codicil of declarant; that we are not directly financially responsible for declarant's medical care; and that we are not agents of any health-care facility in which the declarant may be a patient at the time of signing this directive.

_____

Signature of Witness

_____

Signature of Witness

Washington State Health Care Directive

Directive made this_____day of _____(month, year).

I_____, having the capacity to make health-care decisions, willfully, and voluntarily make known my desire that my dying shall not be artificially prolonged under the circumstances set forth below, and do hereby declare that:

(a) If at any time I should be diagnosed in writing to be in a terminal condition by the attending physician, or in a permanent unconscious condition by two physicians, and where the application of life-sustaining treatment would serve only to artificially prolong the process of my dying, I direct that such treatment be withheld or withdrawn, and that I be permitted to die naturally. I understand by using this form that a terminal condition means an incurable and irreversible condition caused by injury, disease, or illness, that would within reasonable medical judgment cause death within a reasonable period of time in accordance with accepted medical standards, and where the application of life-sustaining treatment would serve only to prolong the process of dying. I further understand in using this form that a permanent unconscious condition means an incurable and irreversible condition in which I am medically assessed within reasonable medical judgment as having no reasonable probability of recovery from an irreversible coma or a persistent vegetative state.

(b) In the absence of my ability to give directions regarding the use of such life-sustaining treatment, it is my intention that this directive shall be honored by my family and physician(s) as the final expression of my legal right to refuse medical or surgical treatment and I accept the consequences of such refusal. If another person is appointed to make these decisions for me, whether through a durable power of attorney or otherwise, I request that the person be guided by this directive and any other clear expressions of my desires.

(c) If I am diagnosed to be in a terminal condition or in a permanent unconscious condition (check one):

_____ I DO want to have artificially provided nutrition and hydration.

_____ I DO NOT want to have artificially provided nutrition and hydration.

(d) If I have been diagnosed as pregnant and that diagnosis is known to my physician, this directive shall have no force or effect during the course of my pregnancy.

(e) I understand the full import of this directive and I am emotionally and mentally capable to make the health-care decisions contained in this directive.

(f) I understand that before I sign this directive, I can add to or delete from or otherwise change the wording of this directive and that I may add to or delete from this directive at any time and that any changes shall be consistent with Washington state law or federal constitutional law to be legally valid.

(g) It is my wish that every part of this directive be fully implemented. If for any reason any part is held invalid it is my wish that the remainder of my directive be implemented.

Signed _____

City, County, and State of Residence _____

The declarer has been personally known to me and I believe him or her to be capable of making health-care decisions.

Witness _____

Witness _____

Sample Forms:

Health-Care Powers of Attorney

The sample forms following are suggested by the laws of those states that allow health-care powers of attorney. See the previous section for forms for living wills and the following section for forms that combine living wills and powers of attorney in some way.

Again, remember that the laws concerning powers of attorney are changing frequently and you must check that you have the most recent form before you fill one out.

Forms for the following states are included in this section:

- Arizona
- Florida
- New York
- South Carolina
- Utah
- Texas

Arizona Health-Care Power of Attorney

1. Health-Care Power of Attorney

I, _____, as principal, designate _____as my agent for all matters relating to my health care, including, without limitation, full power to give or refuse consent to all medical, surgical, hospital and related health care. This power of attorney is effective on my inability to make or communicate health-care decisions. All of my agent's actions under this power during any period when I am unable to make or communicate health-care decisions or when there is uncertainty whether I am dead or alive have the same effect on my heirs, devisees, and personal representatives as if I were alive, competent, and acting for myself.

If my agent is unwilling or unable to serve or continue to serve, I hereby appoint _____as my agent.

I have _____ I have not _____ completed and attached a living will for purposes of providing specific direction to my agent in situations that may occur during any period when I am unable to make or communicate health-care decisions or after my death. My agent is directed to implement those choices I have initialed in the living will.

I have _____ I have not _____ completed a prehospital medical care directive pursuant to § 36-3251, Arizona Revised Statutes.

This health-care directive is made under § 36-3221, Arizona Revised Statutes, and continues in effect for all who may rely on it except those to whom I have given notice of its revocation.

_____
      Signature of Principal

Witness: _____

Date: _____Time:_____

Address:_____

Address of Agent: _____

Witness: _____

Telephone of Agent:_____

Address:_____

(Note: This document may be notarized instead of being witnessed.)

2. Autopsy (under Arizona law an autopsy may be required)

If you wish to do so, reflect your desires below:

_____1. I do not consent to an autopsy.

_____2. I consent to an autopsy.

_____3. My agent may give consent to or refuse an autopsy.

3. Organ Donation (Optional)

(Under Arizona law, you may make a gift of all or part of your body to a bank or storage facility or a hospital, physician, or medical or dental school for transplantation, therapy, medical or dental evaluation or research or for the advancement of medical or dental science. You may also authorize your agent to do so or a member of your family may make a gift unless you give them notice that you do not want a gift made. In the space below, you may make a gift yourself or state that you do not want to make a gift. If you do not complete this section, your agent will have the authority to make a gift of a part of your body pursuant to law. **Note:** The donation elections you make in this health-care power of attorney survive your death.)

If any of the statements below reflects your desire, initial on the line next to that statement. You do not have to initial any of the statements.

If you do not check any of the statements, your agent and your family will have the authority to make a gift of all or part of your body under Arizona law.

_____ I do not want to make an organ or tissue donation and I do not want my agent or family to do so.

_____ I have already signed a written agreement or donor card regarding organ and tissue donation with the following individual or institution: _____

_____ Pursuant to Arizona law, I hereby give, effective on my death:

[ ] Any needed organ or parts.

[ ] The following part or organs listed:

_____

_____

_____

for (check one):

[ ] Any legally authorized purpose.

[ ] Transplant or therapeutic purposes only.

4. Physician Affidavit (optional)

(Before initialing any choices above you may wish to ask questions of your physician regarding a particular treatment alternative. If you do speak with your physician, it is a good idea to ask your physician to complete this affidavit and keep a copy for his or her file.)

I, Dr._____ have reviewed this guidance document and have discussed with_____ any questions regarding the probable medical consequences of the treatment choices provided above. This discussion with the principal occurred on _____(date).

I have agreed to comply with the provisions of this directive.

_____
    Signature of Physician

Florida Designation of Health-Care Surrogate

Name: (Last)_____(First) _____(Middle Initial) _____.

In the event that I have been determined to be incapacitated to provide informed consent for medical treatment and surgical and diagnostic procedures, I wish to designate as my surrogate for health-care decisions:

Name: _____

Address: _____

_____Zip Code:_____.

Phone: _____

If my surrogate is unwilling or unable to perform his or her duties, I wish to designate as my alternate surrogate:

Name: _____

Address: _____

_____Zip Code:_____.

Phone: _____

I fully understand that this designation will permit my designee to make health-care decisions, except for anatomical gifts, unless I have executed an anatomical gift declaration pursuant to law, and to provide, withhold, or withdraw consent on my behalf; to apply for public benefits to defray the cost of health care; and to authorize my admission to or transfer from a health-care facility.

Additional instructions (optional): _____

_____

_____

_____.

I further affirm that this designation is not being made as a condition of treatment or admission to a health-care facility. I will notify and send a copy of this document to the following persons other than my surrogate, so they may know who my surrogate is.

Name: _____

Name: _____

Signed: _____

Date: _____

Witnesses: 1. _____

2. _____

New York Health-Care Proxy

I,_____(name of principal)
hereby appoint _____
(name, home address and telephone number of agent) as my health-care agent to make any
and all health-care decisions for me, except to the extent I state otherwise.

This health-care proxy shall take effect in the event I become unable to make my own
health-care decisions.

NOTE: Although not necessary, and neither encouraged nor discouraged, you may
wish to state instructions or wishes, and limit your agent's authority. Unless your agent
knows your wishes about artificial nutrition and hydration, your agent will not have authority to decide about artificial nutrition and hydration. If you choose to state instructions,
wishes, or limits, please do so below:

_____

_____

_____

I direct my agent to make health-care decisions in accordance with my wishes and instructions as stated above or as otherwise known to him or her. I also direct my agent to
abide by any limitations on his or her authority as stated above or as otherwise known to
him or her.

In the event the person I appoint above is unable, unwilling, or unavailable to act as my
health-care agent, I hereby appoint _____
(name, home address, and telephone number of alternate agent) as my health-care agent.

I understand that, unless I revoke it, this proxy will remain in effect indefinitely or until
the date or occurrence of the condition I have stated below:

(Please complete the following if you do NOT want this health-care proxy to be in effect indefinitely):

This proxy shall expire: (Specify date or condition) _____

Signature:_____

Address: _____

Date: _____

I declare that the person who signed or asked another to sign this document is personally known to me and appears to be of sound mind and acting willingly and free from duress. He or she signed (or asked another to sign for him or her) this document in my presence and that person signed in my presence. I am not the person appointed as agent by this document.

Witness: _____

Address: _____

Witness: _____

Address: _____

South Carolina Declaration of a Desire for a Natural Death

STATE OF SOUTH CAROLINA

COUNTY OF _____

I, _____, Declarant, being at least 18 years of age and a resident of and domiciled in the City of _____, County of_____, State of South Carolina, make this Declaration this _____ day of _____, 20_____.

I wilfully and voluntarily make known my desire that no life-sustaining procedures be used to prolong my dying if my condition is terminal or if I am in a state of permanent unconsciousness, and I declare:

If at any time I have a condition certified to be a terminal condition by two physicians who have personally examined me, one of whom is my attending physician, and the physicians have determined that my death could occur within a reasonably short period of time without the use of life-sustaining procedures or if the physicians certify that I am in a state of permanent unconsciousness and where the application of life-sustaining procedures would serve only to prolong the dying process, I direct that the procedures be withheld or withdrawn, and that I be permitted to die naturally with only the administration of medication or the performance of any medical procedure necessary to provide me with comfort care.

INSTRUCTIONS CONCERNING ARTIFICIAL NUTRITION AND HYDRATION

INITIAL ONE OF THE FOLLOWING STATEMENTS

If my condition is terminal and could result in death within a reasonably short time,

_____ I direct that nutrition and hydration BE PROVIDED through any medically indicated means, including medically or surgically implanted tubes.

_____ I direct that nutrition and hydration NOT BE PROVIDED through any medically indicated means, including medically or surgically implanted tubes.

INITIAL ONE OF THE FOLLOWING STATEMENTS

If I am in a persistent vegetative state or other condition of permanent unconsciousness,

_____ I direct that nutrition and hydration BE PROVIDED through any medically indicated means, including medically or surgically implanted tubes.

_____ I direct that nutrition and hydration NOT BE PROVIDED through any medically indicated means, including medically or surgically implanted tubes.

In the absence of my ability to give directions regarding the use of life-sustaining procedures, it is my intention that this Declaration be honored by my family and physicians and any health facility in which I may be a patient as the final expression of my legal right to refuse medical or surgical treatment, and I accept the consequences from the refusal.

I am aware that this Declaration authorizes a physician to withhold or withdraw life-sustaining procedures. I am emotionally and mentally competent to make this Declaration.

APPOINTMENT OF AN AGENT (OPTIONAL)

1. You may give another person authority to revoke this declaration on your behalf. If you wish to do so, please enter that person's name in the space below.

    Name of Agent with Power to Revoke:_____

    Address: _____

    Telephone Number: _____

2. You may give another person authority to enforce this declaration on your behalf. If you wish to do so, please enter that person's name in the space below.

    Name of Agent with Power to Enforce: _____

    Address: _____

    Telephone Number: _____

REVOCATION PROCEDURES

THIS DECLARATION MAY BE REVOKED BY ANY ONE OF THE FOLLOWING METHODS. HOWEVER, A REVOCATION IS NOT EFFECTIVE UNTIL IT IS COMMUNICATED TO THE ATTENDING PHYSICIAN.

(1) BY BEING DEFACED, TORN, OBLITERATED, OR OTHERWISE DESTROYED, IN EXPRESSION OF YOUR INTENT TO REVOKE, BY YOU OR BY SOME PERSON IN YOUR PRESENCE AND BY YOUR DIRECTION. REVOCATION BY DESTRUCTION OF ONE OR MORE OF MULTIPLE ORIGINAL DECLARATIONS REVOKES ALL OF THE ORIGINAL DECLARATIONS;

(2) BY A WRITTEN REVOCATION SIGNED AND DATED BY YOU EXPRESSING YOUR INTENT TO REVOKE;

(3) BY YOUR ORAL EXPRESSION OF YOUR INTENT TO REVOKE THE DECLA-RATION. AN ORAL REVOCATION COMMUNICATED TO THE ATTENDING PHYSICIAN BY A PERSON OTHER THAN YOU IS EFFECTIVE ONLY IF:

   (a) THE PERSON WAS PRESENT WHEN THE ORAL REVOCATION WAS MADE;

   (b) THE REVOCATION WAS COMMUNICATED TO THE PHYSICIAN WITHIN A REASONABLE TIME;

   (c) YOUR PHYSICAL OR MENTAL CONDITION MAKES IT IMPOSSIBLE FOR THE PHYSICIAN TO CONFIRM THROUGH SUBSEQUENT CONVERSA-TION WITH YOU THAT THE REVOCATION HAS OCCURRED.

   TO BE EFFECTIVE AS A REVOCATION, THE ORAL EXPRESSION CLEARLY MUST INDICATE YOUR DESIRE THAT THE DECLARATION NOT BE GIVEN EFFECT OR THAT LIFE-SUSTAINING PROCEDURES BE ADMINISTERED;

(4) IF YOU, IN THE SPACE ABOVE, HAVE AUTHORIZED AN AGENT TO RE-VOKE THE DECLARATION, THE AGENT MAY REVOKE ORALLY OR BY A WRITTEN, SIGNED, AND DATED INSTRUMENT. AN AGENT MAY REVOKE ONLY IF YOU ARE INCOMPETENT TO DO SO. AN AGENT MAY REVOKE THE DECLARATION PERMANENTLY OR TEMPORARILY.

(5) BY YOUR EXECUTING ANOTHER DECLARATION AT A LATER TIME.

_____
   Signature of Declarant

AFFIDAVIT

STATE OF _____

COUNTY OF _____

We, _____ and _____, the undersigned witnesses to the foregoing Declaration, dated the _____ day of_____, 20 ___, at least one of us being first duly sworn, declare to the undersigned authority, on the basis of our best information and belief, that the Declaration was on that date signed by the declarant as and for his or her DECLARATION OF A DESIRE FOR A NATURAL DEATH in our presence and we, at his or her request and in his or her presence, and in the presence of each other, subscribe our names as witnesses on that date. The declarant is personally known to us, and we know him or her to be of sound mind. Each of us affirms that he or she is qualified as a witness to this Declaration under the provisions of the South Carolina Death With Dignity Act in that he or she is not related to the declarant by blood, marriage, or adoption, either as a spouse, lineal ancestor, descendant of the parents of the declarant, or spouse of any of them; nor directly financially responsible for the declarant's medical care; nor entitled to any portion of the declarant's estate upon his or her decease, whether under any will or as an heir by intestate succession; nor the beneficiary of a life insurance policy of the declarant; nor the declarant's attending physician; nor an employee of the attending physician; nor a person who has a claim against the declarant's decedent's estate as of this time. No more than one of us is an employee of a health facility in which the declarant is a patient. If the declarant is a resident in a hospital or nursing care facility at the date of execution of this Declaration, at least one of us is an ombudsman designated by the State Ombudsman, Office of the Governor.

_____Witness

_____Witness

Subscribed before me by_____, the declarant, and subscribed and sworn to before me by_____, the witnesses, this_____ day of _____, 20____.

_____
          Signature

Notary Public for _____

My commission expires: _____

SEAL

Utah Special Power of Attorney

I, _____, of _____ , this_____day of _____, _____, being of sound mind, willfully and voluntarily appoint _____ of _____ as my agent and attorney-in-fact, without substitution, with lawful authority to execute a directive on my behalf under Section 75-2-1105, governing the care and treatment to be administered to or withheld from me at any time after I incur an injury, disease, or illness which renders me unable to give current directions to attending physicians and other providers of medical services.

I have carefully selected my above-named agent with confidence in the belief that this person's familiarity with my desires, beliefs, and attitudes will result in directions to attending physicians and providers of medical services which would probably be the same as I would give if able to do so.

This power of attorney shall be and remain in effect from the time my attending physician certifies that I have incurred a physical or mental condition rendering me unable to give current directions to attending physicians and other providers of medical services as to my care and treatment.

_____
     Signature of Principal

State of _____)

               : ss.

County of_____)

On the _____ day of_____,_____, personally appeared before me _____, who duly acknowledged to me that he or she has read and fully understands the foregoing power of attorney, executed the same of his or her own volition and for the purposes set forth, and that he or she was acting under no constraint or undue influence whatsoever.

_____
     Notary Public

My commission expires: Residing at:_____

_____

Texas Medical Power of Attorney Designation of Health-Care Agent

I, _____(insert your name) appoint:

Name: _____

Address: _____

Phone: _____

as my agent to make any and all health-care decisions for me, except to the extent I state otherwise in this document. This medical power of attorney takes effect if I become unable to make my own health-care decisions and this fact is certified in writing by my physician.

LIMITATIONS ON THE DECISION-MAKING AUTHORITY OF MY AGENT ARE AS FOLLOWS: _____

_____

DESIGNATION OF ALTERNATE AGENT.

(You are not required to designate an alternate agent but you may do so. An alternate agent may make the same health-care decisions as the designated agent if the designated agent is unable or unwilling to act as your agent. If the agent designated is your spouse, the designation is automatically revoked by law if your marriage is dissolved.)

If the person designated as my agent is unable or unwilling to make health-care decisions for me, I designate the following persons to serve as my agent to make health-care decisions for me as authorized by this document, who serve in the following order:

A. First Alternate Agent

Name:_____

Address:_____ Phone:_____

B. Second Alternate Agent

Name:_____

Address:_____ Phone:_____

The original of this document is kept at:

_____

_____

_____

The following individuals or institutions have signed copies:

Name: _____

Address: _____

_____

Name: _____

Address: _____

_____

DURATION

I understand that this power of attorney exists indefinitely from the date I execute this document unless I establish a shorter time or revoke the power of attorney. If I am unable to make health-care decisions for myself when this power of attorney expires, the authority I have granted my agent continues to exist until the time I become able to make health-care decisions for myself.

(IF APPLICABLE) This power of attorney ends on the following date: _____

PRIOR DESIGNATIONS REVOKED.

I revoke any prior medical power of attorney.

ACKNOWLEDGMENT OF DISCLOSURE STATEMENT.

I have been provided with a disclosure statement explaining the effect of this document. I have read and understand that information contained in the disclosure statement.

(YOU MUST DATE AND SIGN THIS POWER OF ATTORNEY.)

I sign my name to this medical power of attorney on ___ day of _____ (month, year) at_____ (City and State)

_____
Signature

_____
(Print Name)

STATEMENT OF FIRST WITNESS.

I am not the person appointed as agent by this document. I am not related to the principal by blood or marriage. I would not be entitled to any portion of the principal's estate on the principal's death. I am not the attending physician of the principal or an employee of the attending physician. I have no claim against any portion of the principal's estate on the principal's death. Furthermore, if I am an employee of a health-care facility in which the principal is a patient, I am not involved in providing direct patient care to the principal and am not an officer, director, partner, or business office employee of the health-care facility or of any parent organization of the health-care facility.

Signature: _____ Date: _____

Print Name: _____

Address: _____

STATEMENT OF SECOND WITNESS.

I am not the person appointed as agent by this document. I am not related to the principal by blood or marriage. I would not be entitled to any portion of the principal's estate on the principal's death. I am not the attending physician of the principal or an employee of the attending physician. I have no claim against any portion of the principal's estate on the principal's death. Furthermore, if I am an employee of a health-care facility in which the principal is a patient, I am not involved in providing direct patient care to the principal and am not an officer, director, partner, or business office employee of the health-care facility or of any parent organization of the health-care facility.

Signature: _____ Date: _____

Print Name: _____

Address: _____

Sample Forms:

Combined Forms

The sample forms following are suggested by the laws of those states that allow forms that combine living wills with powers of attorney in some way. Always remember that the laws concerning living wills powers of attorney are changing frequently and you must check that you have the most recent form before you fill one out.

Included in this section are forms for the following states:

- California
- Connecticut
- Illinois
- Maryland
- Virginia

California Advance Health-Care Directive

(California Probate Code Section 4701)

Explanation

You have the right to give instructions about your own health care. You also have the right to name someone else to make health-care decisions for you. This form lets you do either or both of these things. It also lets you express your wishes regarding donation of organs and the designation of your primary physician. If you use this form, you may complete or modify all or any part of it. You are free to use a different form.

Part 1 of this form is a power of attorney for health care. Part 1 lets you name another individual as agent to make health-care decisions for you if you become incapable of making your own decisions or if you want someone else to make those decisions for you now even though you are still capable. You may also name an alternate agent to act for you if your first choice is not willing, able, or reasonably available to make decisions for you. (Your agent may not be an operator or employee of a community care facility or a residential care facility where you are receiving care, or your supervising health-care provider or employee of the health-care institution where you are receiving care, unless your agent is related to you or is a coworker.)

Unless the form you sign limits the authority of your agent, your agent may make all health-care decisions for you. This form has a place for you to limit the authority of your agent. You need not limit the authority of your agent if you wish to rely on your agent for all health-care decisions that may have to be made. If you choose not to limit the authority of your agent, your agent will have the right to:

(a) Consent or refuse consent to any care, treatment, service, or procedure to maintain, diagnose, or otherwise affect a physical or mental condition.

(b) Select or discharge health-care providers and institutions.

(c) Approve or disapprove diagnostic tests, surgical procedures, and programs of medication.

(d) Direct the provision, withholding, or withdrawal of artificial nutrition and hydration and all other forms of health-care, including cardiopulmonary resuscitation.

(e) Make anatomical gifts, authorize an autopsy, and direct disposition of remains.

Part 2 of this form lets you give specific instructions about any aspect of your health care, whether or not you appoint an agent. Choices are provided for you to express your wishes regarding the provision, withholding, or withdrawal of treatment to keep you alive, as well as the provision of pain relief. Space is also provided for you to add to the choices you have made or for you to write out any additional wishes. If you are satisfied to allow your agent to determine what is best for you in making end-of-life decisions, you need not fill out Part 2 of this form.

Part 3 of this form lets you express an intention to donate your bodily organs and tissues following your death.

Part 4 of this form lets you designate a physician to have primary responsibility for your health care.

After completing this form, sign and date the form at the end. The form must be signed by two qualified witnesses or acknowledged before a notary public. Give a copy of the signed and completed form to your physician, to any other health-care providers you may have, to any health-care institution at which you are receiving care, and to any health-care agents you have named. You should talk to the person you have named as agent to make sure that he or she understands your wishes and is willing to take the responsibility.

You have the right to revoke this advance health-care directive or replace this form at any time.

PART 1

POWER OF ATTORNEY FOR HEALTH CARE

(1.1) DESIGNATION OF AGENT: I designate the following individual as my agent to make health-care decisions for me: _____

(name of individual you choose as agent)

_____	_____	_____	_____
(address)	(city)	(state)	(ZIP Code)

_____	_____
(home phone)	(work phone)

OPTIONAL: If I revoke my agent's authority or if my agent is not willing, able, or reasonably available to make a health-care decision for me, I designate as my first alternate agent:

_____

(name of individual you choose as first alternate agent)

_____	_____	_____	_____
(address)	(city)	(state)	(ZIP Code)

_____	_____
(home phone)	(work phone)

OPTIONAL: If I revoke the authority of my agent and first alternate agent or if neither is willing, able, or reasonably available to make a health-care decision for me, I designate as my second alternate agent:

_____

(name of individual you choose as second alternate agent)

_____

(address)   (city)   (state)   (ZIP Code)

_____

(home phone)   (work phone)

(1.2) AGENT'S AUTHORITY: My agent is authorized to make all health-care decisions for me, including decisions to provide, withhold, or withdraw artificial nutrition and hydration and all other forms of health care to keep me alive, except as I state here:

_____

_____

_____

(Add additional sheets if needed.)

(1.3) WHEN AGENT'S AUTHORITY BECOMES EFFECTIVE: My agent's authority becomes effective when my primary physician determines that I am unable to make my own health-care decisions unless I mark the following box. If I mark this box [_], my agent's authority to make health-care decisions for me takes effect immediately.

(1.4) AGENT'S OBLIGATION: My agent shall make health-care decisions for me in accordance with this power of attorney for health care, any instructions I give in Part 2 of this form, and my other wishes to the extent known to my agent. To the extent my wishes are unknown, my agent shall make health-care decisions for me in accordance with what my agent determines to be in my best interest. In determining my best interest, my agent shall consider my personal values to the extent known to my agent.

(1.5) AGENT'S POSTDEATH AUTHORITY: My agent is authorized to make anatomical gifts, authorize an autopsy, and direct disposition of my remains, except as I state here or in Part 3 of this form:

_____

_____

_____

(Add additional sheets if needed.)

(1.6)   NOMINATION OF CONSERVATOR: If a conservator of my person needs to be appointed for me by a court, I nominate the agent designated in this form. If that agent is not willing, able, or reasonably available to act as conservator, I nominate the alternate agents whom I have named, in the order designated.

PART 2

INSTRUCTIONS FOR HEALTH CARE

If you fill out this part of the form, you may strike any wording you do not want.

(2.1)   END-OF-LIFE DECISIONS: I direct that my health-care providers and others involved in my care provide, withhold, or withdraw treatment in accordance with the choice I have marked below:

> [ ] (a) Choice Not To Prolong Life. I do not want my life to be prolonged if (1) I have an incurable and irreversible condition that will result in my death within a relatively short time, (2) I become unconscious and, to a reasonable degree of medical certainty, I will not regain consciousness, or (3) the likely risks and burdens of treatment would outweigh the expected benefits, OR

> [ ] (b) Choice To Prolong Life. I want my life to be prolonged as long as possible within the limits of generally accepted health-care standards.

(2.2)   RELIEF FROM PAIN: Except as I state in the following space, I direct that treatment for alleviation of pain or discomfort be provided at all times, even if it hastens my death:

_____

_____

_____

(Add additional sheets if needed.)

(2.3)   OTHER WISHES: (If you do not agree with any of the optional choices above and wish to write your own, or if you wish to add to the instructions you have given above, you may do so here.) I direct that:

_____

_____

_____

(Add additional sheets if needed.)

PART 3

DONATION OF ORGANS AT DEATH

(OPTIONAL)

(3.1)   Upon my death (mark applicable box):

[ ] (a) I give any needed organs, tissues, or parts, OR

[ ] (b) I give the following organs, tissues, or parts only:

_____

[ ] (c) My gift is for the following purposes (strike any of the following you do not want):

(1) Transplant

(2) Therapy

(3) Research

(4) Education

PART 4

PRIMARY PHYSICIAN

(OPTIONAL)

(4.1)   I designate the following physician as my primary physician:

_____
(name of physician)

_____
(address)   (city)   (state)   (ZIP Code)

_____
(home phone)   (work phone)

OPTIONAL: If the physician I have designated above is not willing, able, or reasonably available to act as my primary physician, I designate the following physician as my primary physician:

_____
(name of physician)

(address)	(city)	(state)	(ZIP Code)

(home phone)	(work phone)

PART 5

(5.1)   EFFECT OF COPY: A copy of this form has the same effect as the original.

(5.2)   SIGNATURE: Sign and date the form here:

_____	_____
(date)	(sign your name)
_____	_____
(address)	(print your name)
_____	
(city) (state)	

(5.3)   STATEMENT OF WITNESSES: I declare under penalty of perjury under the laws of California (1) that the individual who signed or acknowledged this advance health-care directive is personally known to me, or that the individual's identity was proven to me by convincing evidence, (2) that the individual signed or acknowledged this advance directive in my presence, (3) that the individual appears to be of sound mind and under no duress, fraud, or undue influence, (4) that I am not a person appointed as agent by this advance directive, and (5) that I am not the individual's health-care provider, an employee of the individual's health-care provider, the operator of a community care facility, an employee of an operator of a community care facility, the operator of a residential care facility for the elderly, nor an employee of an operator of a residential care facility for the elderly.

First witness	Second witness
_____	_____
(print name)	(print name)
_____	_____
(address)	(address)
_____	_____
(city) (state)	(city) (state)

_____   _____
(signature of witness)   (signature of witness)

_____   _____
(date)   (date)

(5.4) ADDITIONAL STATEMENT OF WITNESSES: At least one of the above witnesses must also sign the following declaration:

I further declare under penalty of perjury under the laws of California that I am not related to the individual executing this advance health-care directive by blood, marriage, or adoption, and to the best of my knowledge, I am not entitled to any part of the individual's estate upon his or her death under a will now existing or by operation of law.

_____   _____
(signature of witness)   (signature of witness)

PART 6

SPECIAL WITNESS REQUIREMENT

(6.1) The following statement is required only if you are a patient in a skilled nursing facility — a health care facility that provides the following basic services: skilled nursing care and supportive care to patients whose primary need is for availability of skilled nursing care on an extended basis. The patient advocate or ombudsman must sign the following statement:

STATEMENT OF PATIENT ADVOCATE OR OMBUDSMAN

I declare under penalty of perjury under the laws of California that I am a patient advocate or ombudsman as designated by the State Department of Aging and that I am serving as a witness as required by Section 4675 of the Probate Code.

_____   _____
(date)   (sign your name)

_____   _____
(address)   (print your name)

_____
(city)   (state)

Connecticut

THESE ARE MY HEALTH-CARE INSTRUCTIONS.

MY APPOINTMENT OF A HEALTH-CARE AGENT,

MY APPOINTMENT OF AN ATTORNEY-IN-FACT

FOR HEALTH-CARE DECISIONS,

THE DESIGNATION OF MY CONSERVATOR OF THE PERSON

FOR MY FUTURE INCAPACITY

AND

MY DOCUMENT OF ANATOMICAL GIFT

To any physician who is treating me: These are my health-care instructions including those concerning the withholding or withdrawal of life support systems, together with the appointment of my health-care agent and my attorney-in-fact for health-care decisions, the designation of my conservator of the person for future incapacity and my document of anatomical gift. As my physician, you may rely on any decision made by my health-care agent, attorney-in-fact for health care decisions, or conservator of my person, if I am unable to make a decision for myself.

I, _____, the author of this document, request that, if my condition is deemed terminal or if I am determined to be permanently unconscious, I be allowed to die and not be kept alive through life support systems. By terminal condition, I mean that I have an incurable or irreversible medical condition which, without the administration of life support systems, will, in the opinion of my attending physician, result in death within a relatively short time. By permanently unconscious I mean that I am in a permanent coma or persistent vegetative state which is an irreversible condition in which I am at no time aware of myself or the environment and show no behavioral response to the environment. The life support systems which I do not want to include, but are not limited to: artificial respiration, cardiopulmonary resuscitation and artificial means of providing nutrition and hydration. I do want sufficient pain medication to maintain my physical comfort. I do not intend any direct taking of my life, but only that my dying not be unreasonably prolonged.

I appoint _____to be my health-care agent and my attorney-in-fact for health-care decisions. If my attending physician determines that I am unable to understand and appreciate the nature and consequences of health-care decisions and unable to reach and communicate an informed decision regarding treatment, my health-care agent and attorney-in-fact for health-care decisions is authorized to:

(1) Convey to my physician my wishes concerning the withholding or removal of life support systems;

(2) Take whatever actions are necessary to ensure that any wishes are given effect;

(3) Consent, refuse, or withdraw consent to any medical treatment as long as such action is consistent with my wishes concerning the withholding or removal of life support systems; and

(4) Consent to any medical treatment designed solely for the purpose of maintaining physical comfort.

If _____ is unwilling or unable to serve as my health-care agent and my attorney-in-fact for health-care decisions, I appoint _____ _____to be my alternative health-care agent and my attorney-in-fact for health-care decisions.

If a conservator of my person should need to be appointed, I designate _____ _____be appointed my conservator. If _____ is unwilling or unable to serve as my conservator, I designate _____. No bond shall be required of either of them in any jurisdiction.

I hereby make this anatomical gift, if medically acceptable, to take effect upon my death.

I give: (check one)

_____(1) any needed organs or parts

_____(2) only the following organs or parts, _____

_____

_____

_____to be donated for: (check one)

_____(1) any of the purposes stated in subsection (a) of section 19a-279f of the general statutes;

_____(2) these limited purposes: _____

_____

_____.

These requests, appointments, and designations are made after careful reflection, while I am of sound mind. Any party receiving a duly executed copy or facsimile of this document may rely upon it unless such party has received actual notice of my revocation of it.

Date _____, _____ _____L.S.

This document was signed in our presence by _____ the author of this document, who appeared to be 18 years of age or older, of sound mind, and able to understand the nature and consequences of health-care decisions at the time this document was signed. The author appeared to be under no improper influence. We have subscribed this document in the author's presence and at the author's request and in the presence of each other.

_____   _____
(Witness)   (Witness)

_____   _____
(Number and Street)   (Number and Street)

_____   _____
(City, State, and Zip Code)   (City, State, and Zip Code)

STATE OF CONNECTICUT)

) ss. ....

COUNTY OF _____)

We, the subscribing witnesses, being duly sworn, say that we witnessed the execution of these health-care instructions, the appointments of a health-care agent and an attorney-in-fact, the designation of a conservator for future incapacity and a document of anatomical gift by the author of this document; that the author subscribed, published, and declared the same to be the author's instructions, appointments, and designation in our presence; that we thereafter subscribed the document as witnesses in the author's presence, at the author's request, and in the presence of each other; that at the time of the execution of said document the author appeared to us to be 18 years of age or older, of sound mind, able to understand the nature and consequences of said document, and under no improper influence, and we make this affidavit at the author's request this _____ day of

_____.

_____   _____
(Witness)   (Witness)

Subscribed and sworn to before me this _____ day of _____, ____.

Commissioner of the Superior Court

Notary Public

My commission expires:_____.

(Print or type name of all persons signing under all signatures.)

Illinois Statutory Short Form Power of Attorney for Health Care

NOTICE: THE PURPOSE OF THIS POWER OF ATTORNEY IS TO GIVE THE PERSON YOU DESIGNATE (YOUR "AGENT") BROAD POWERS TO MAKE HEALTH-CARE DE- CISIONS FOR YOU, INCLUDING POWER TO REQUIRE, CONSENT TO OR WITH- DRAW ANY TYPE OF PERSONAL CARE OR MEDICAL TREATMENT FOR ANY PHYSICAL OR MENTAL CONDITION AND TO ADMIT YOU TO OR DISCHARGE YOU FROM ANY HOSPITAL, HOME, OR OTHER INSTITUTION. THIS FORM DOES NOT IMPOSE A DUTY ON YOUR AGENT TO EXERCISE GRANTED POWERS; BUT WHEN POWERS ARE EXERCISED, YOUR AGENT WILL HAVE TO USE DUE CARE TO ACT FOR YOUR BENEFIT AND IN ACCORDANCE WITH THIS FORM AND KEEP A RECORD OF RECEIPTS, DISBURSEMENTS, AND SIGNIFICANT ACTIONS TAKEN AS AGENT. A COURT CAN TAKE AWAY THE POWERS OF YOUR AGENT IF IT FINDS THE AGENT IS NOT ACTING PROPERLY. YOU MAY NAME SUCCESSOR AGENTS UNDER THIS FORM BUT NOT CO-AGENTS, AND NO HEALTH-CARE PROVIDER MAY BE NAMED. UNLESS YOU EXPRESSLY LIMIT THE DURATION OF THIS POWER IN THE MANNER PROVIDED BELOW, UNTIL YOU REVOKE THIS POWER OR A COURT ACTING ON YOUR BEHALF TERMINATES IT, YOUR AGENT MAY EXERCISE THE POWERS GIVEN HERE THROUGHOUT YOUR LIFETIME, EVEN AFTER YOU BE- COME DISABLED. THE POWERS YOU GIVE YOUR AGENT, YOUR RIGHT TO RE- VOKE THOSE POWERS, AND THE PENALTIES FOR VIOLATING THE LAW ARE EXPLAINED MORE FULLY IN SECTIONS 4-5, 4-6, 4-9, AND 4-10(b) OF THE ILLINOIS "POWERS OF ATTORNEY FOR HEALTH-CARE LAW" OF WHICH THIS FORM IS A PART (SEE THE BACK OF THIS FORM). THAT LAW EXPRESSLY PERMITS THE USE OF ANY DIFFERENT FORM OF POWER OF ATTORNEY YOU MAY DESIRE. IF THERE IS ANYTHING ABOUT THIS FORM THAT YOU DO NOT UNDERSTAND, YOU SHOULD ASK A LAWYER TO EXPLAIN IT TO YOU.)

POWER OF ATTORNEY made this _____ day of_____
                                                        (month) (year)

1. I, _____(name),
   _____(address)
   hereby appoint: _____
   (insert name and address of agent), as my attorney-in-fact (my "agent") to act for me and in my name (in any way I could act in person) to make any and all decisions for me concerning my personal care, medical treatment, hospitalization, and health care and to require, withhold, or withdraw any type of medical treatment or procedure, even though my death may ensue. My agent shall have the same access to my medical

records that I have, including the right to disclose the contents to others. My agent shall also have full power to authorize an autopsy and direct the disposition of my remains. Effective upon my death, my agent has the full power to make an anatomical gift of the following (initial one):

_____ Any organ.

_____ Specific organs: _____.

(THE ABOVE GRANT OF POWER IS INTENDED TO BE AS BROAD AS POSSIBLE SO THAT YOUR AGENT WILL HAVE AUTHORITY TO MAKE ANY DECISION YOU COULD MAKE TO OBTAIN OR TERMINATE ANY TYPE OF HEALTH CARE, INCLUDING WITHDRAWAL OF FOOD AND WATER AND OTHER LIFE-SUSTAINING MEASURES, IF YOUR AGENT BELIEVES SUCH ACTION WOULD BE CONSISTENT WITH YOUR INTENT AND DESIRES. IF YOU WISH TO LIMIT THE SCOPE OF YOUR AGENT'S POWERS OR PRESCRIBE SPECIAL RULES OR LIMIT THE POWER TO MAKE AN ANATOMICAL GIFT, AUTHORIZE AUTOPSY, OR DISPOSE OF REMAINS, YOU MAY DO SO IN THE FOLLOWING PARAGRAPHS.)

2. The powers granted above shall not include the following powers or shall be subject to the following rules or limitations (here you may include any specific limitations you deem appropriate, such as your own definition of when life-sustaining measures should be withheld; a direction to continue food and fluids or life-sustaining treatment in all events; or instructions to refuse any specific types of treatment that are inconsistent with your religious beliefs or unacceptable to you for any other reason, such as blood transfusion, electro-convulsive therapy, amputation, psychosurgery, voluntary admission to a mental institution, etc.):_____

_____

_____

_____.

(THE SUBJECT OF LIFE-SUSTAINING TREATMENT IS OF PARTICULAR IMPORTANCE. FOR YOUR CONVENIENCE IN DEALING WITH THAT SUBJECT, SOME GENERAL STATEMENTS CONCERNING THE WITHHOLDING OR REMOVAL OF LIFE-SUSTAINING TREATMENT ARE SET FORTH BELOW. IF YOU AGREE WITH ONE OF THESE STATEMENTS, YOU MAY INITIAL THAT STATEMENT; BUT DO NOT INITIAL MORE THAN ONE):

I do not want my life to be prolonged nor do I want life-sustaining treatment to be provided or continued if my agent believes the burdens of the treatment outweigh the expected benefits. I want my agent to consider the relief of suffering, the expense involved, and the quality as well as the possible extension of my life in making decisions concerning life-sustaining treatment. Initialed: _____

I want my life to be prolonged and I want life-sustaining treatment to be provided or continued unless I am in a coma which my attending physician believes to be irreversible, in accordance with reasonable medical standards at the time of reference. If and when I have suffered irreversible coma, I want life-sustaining treatment to be withheld or discontinued. Initialed: _____

I want my life to be prolonged to the greatest extent possible without regard to my condition, the chances I have for recovery, or the cost of the procedures. Initialed:_____

(THIS POWER OF ATTORNEY MAY BE AMENDED OR REVOKED BY YOU IN THE MANNER PROVIDED IN SECTION 4-6 OF THE ILLINOIS "POWERS OF ATTORNEY FOR HEALTH-CARE LAW". ABSENT AMENDMENT OR REVOCATION, THE AUTHORITY GRANTED IN THIS POWER OF ATTORNEY WILL BECOME EFFECTIVE AT THE TIME THIS POWER IS SIGNED AND WILL CONTINUE UNTIL YOUR DEATH, AND BEYOND IF ANATOMICAL GIFT, AUTOPSY OR DISPOSITION OF REMAINS IS AUTHORIZED, UNLESS A LIMITATION ON THE BEGINNING DATE OR DURATION IS MADE BY INITIALING AND COMPLETING EITHER OR BOTH OF THE FOLLOWING:)

3. (___) This power of attorney shall become effective on_____
_____(insert a future date or event during your lifetime, such as court determination of your disability, when you want this power to first take effect).

4. (___) This power of attorney shall terminate on _____ (insert a future date or event, such as court determination of your disability, when you want this power to terminate prior to your death).

(IF YOU WISH TO NAME SUCCESSOR AGENTS, INSERT THE NAMES AND ADDRESSES OF SUCH SUCCESSORS IN THE FOLLOWING PARAGRAPH.)

5. If any agent named by me shall die, become incompetent, resign, refuse to accept the office of agent, or be unavailable, I name the following (each to act alone and successively, in the order named) as successors to such agent:_____.
For purposes of this paragraph 5, a person shall be considered to be incompetent if and

while the person is a minor or an adjudicated incompetent or disabled person or the person is unable to give prompt and intelligent consideration to health-care matters, as certified by a licensed physician.

(IF YOU WISH TO NAME YOUR AGENT AS GUARDIAN OF YOUR PERSON, IN THE EVENT A COURT DECIDES THAT ONE SHOULD BE APPOINTED, YOU MAY, BUT ARE NOT REQUIRED TO, DO SO BY RETAINING THE FOLLOWING PARAGRAPH. THE COURT WILL APPOINT YOUR AGENT IF THE COURT FINDS THAT SUCH APPOINTMENT WILL SERVE YOUR BEST INTERESTS AND WELFARE. STRIKE OUT PARAGRAPH 6 IF YOU DO NOT WANT YOUR AGENT TO ACT AS GUARDIAN.)

6. If a guardian of my person is to be appointed, I nominate the agent acting under this power of attorney as such guardian, to serve without bond or security.

7. I am fully informed as to all the contents of this form and understand the full import of this grant of powers to my agent.

Signed:_____
                      (principal)

The principal has had an opportunity to read the above form and has signed the form or acknowledged his or her signature or mark on the form in my presence.

_____Residing at _____
    (witness)

(YOU MAY, BUT ARE NOT REQUIRED TO, REQUEST YOUR AGENT AND SUCCESSOR AGENTS TO PROVIDE SPECIMEN SIGNATURES BELOW. IF YOU INCLUDE SPECIMEN SIGNATURES IN THIS POWER OF ATTORNEY, YOU MUST COMPLETE THE CERTIFICATION OPPOSITE THE SIGNATURES OF THE AGENTS.)

(Specimen signatures of agent and successors)	(I certify that the signatures of my agent and successors are correct.)
_____ (agent)	_____ (principal)
_____ (successor agent)	_____ (principal)
_____ (successor agent)	_____ (principal)

Excerpts from Illinois Powers of Attorney for Health Care Law

Section 4-5. Limitations on health care agencies.

Neither the attending physician nor any other health care provider may act as agent under a health care agency; however, a person who is not administering health care to the patient may act as health care agent for the patient even though the person is a physician or otherwise licensed, certified, authorized, or permitted by law to administer health care in the ordinary course of business or the practice of a profession.

Section 4-6. Revocation and amendment of health care agencies.

(a) Every health care agency may be revoked by the principal at any time, without regard to the principal's mental or physical condition, by any of the following methods:

1. By being obliterated, burnt, torn or otherwise destroyed or defaced in a manner indicating intention to revoke;

2. By a written revocation of the agency signed and dated by the principal or person acting at the direction of the principal; or

3. By an oral or any other expression of the intent to revoke the agency in the presence of a witness 18 years of age or older who signs and dates a writing confirming that such expression of intent was made.

(b) Every health care agency may be amended at any time by a written amendment signed and dated by the principal or person acting at the direction of the principal.

(c) Any person, other than the agent, to whom a revocation or amendment is communicated or delivered shall make all reasonable efforts to inform the agent of that fact as promptly as possible.

Section 4-9. Penalties.

All persons shall be subject to the following sanctions in relation to health care agencies, in addition to all other sanctions applicable under any other law or rule of professional conduct:

(a) Any person shall be civilly liable who, without the principal's consent, willfully conceals, cancels or alters a health care agency or any amendment or revocation of the agency or who falsifies or forges a health care agency, amendment or revocation.

(b) A person who falsifies or forges a health care agency or willfully conceals or withholds personal knowledge of an amendment or revocation of a health care agency with the intent to cause a withholding or withdrawal of life-sustaining or death-delaying procedures contrary to the intent of the principal and thereby, because of such act, directly causes life-sustaining or death-delaying procedures to be withheld or withdrawn and death to the patient to be hastened shall be subject to prosecution for involuntary manslaughter.

(c) Any person who requires or prevents execution of a health care agency as a condition of insuring or providing any type of health care services to the patient shall be civilly liable and guilty of a Class A misdemeanor.

Section 4-10. Statutory short form power of attorney for health care.

(a) Paragraph (a) sets out the form of the statutory health care power that is reproduced on the face of this form.

(b) The statutory short form power of attorney for health care (the "statutory health care power") authorizes the agent to make any and all health care decisions on behalf of the principal which the principal could make if present and under no disability, subject to any limitations on the granted powers that appear on the face of the form, to be exercised in such manner as the agent deems consistent with the intent and desires of the principal. The agent will be under no duty to exercise granted powers or to assume control of or responsibility for the principal's health care; but when granted powers are exercised, the agent will be required to use due care to act for the benefit of the principal in accordance with the terms of the statutory health care power and will be liable for negligent exercise. The agent may act in person or through others reasonably employed by the agent for that purpose but may not delegate authority to make health care decisions. The agent may sign and deliver all instruments, negotiate and enter into all agreements and do all other acts reasonably necessary to implement the exercise of the powers granted to the agent. Without limiting the generality of the foregoing, the statutory health care power shall include the following powers, subject to any limitations appearing on the face of the form:

1. The agent is authorized to give consent to and authorize or refuse, or to withhold or withdraw consent to, any and all types of medical care, treatment or procedures relating to the physical or mental health of the principal, including any medication program, surgical procedures, life-sustaining treatment or provision of food and fluids for the principal.

2. The agent is authorized to admit the principal to or discharge the principal from any and all types of hospitals, institutions, homes, residential or nursing facilities, treatment centers and other health care institutions providing personal care or treatment for any type of physical or mental condition. The agent shall have the same right to visit the principal in the hospital or other institution as is granted to a spouse or adult child of the principal, any rule of the institution to the contrary notwithstanding.

3. The agent is authorized to contract for any and all types of health care services and facilities in the name of and on behalf of the principal and to bind the principal to pay for all such services and facilities, and to have and exercise those powers over the principal's property as are authorized under the statutory property power, to the extent the agent deems necessary to pay health care costs; and the agent shall not be personally liable for any services or care contracted for on behalf of the principal.

4. At the principal's expense and subject to reasonable rules of the health care provider to prevent disruption of the principal's health care, the agent shall have the same right the principal has to examine and copy and consent to disclosure of all the principal's medical records that the agent deems relevant to the exercise of the agent's powers, whether the records relate to mental health or any other medical condition and whether they are in the possession of or maintained by any physician, psychiatrist, psychologist, therapist, hospital, nursing home or other health care provider.

5. The agent is authorized to direct that an autopsy be made pursuant to Section 2 of "An Act in relation to autopsy of dead bodies," approved August 13, 1965, including all amendments; to made a disposition of any part or all of the principal's body pursuant to the Uniform Anatomical Gift Act, as now or hereafter amended; and to direct the disposition of the principal's remains.

Maryland Health-Care Decision Making Forms

The following forms allow you to make some decisions about future health-care issues. Form I, called a "Living Will", allows you to make decisions about life-sustaining procedures if, in the future, your death from a terminal condition is imminent despite the application of life-sustaining procedures or you are in a persistent vegetative state. Form II, called an "Advance Directive," allows you to select a health-care agent, give healthcare instructions, or both. If you use the advance directive, you can make decisions about life-sustaining procedures in the event of terminal condition, persistent vegetative state, or end-stage condition. You can also use the advance directive to make any other health-care decisions.

These forms are intended to be guides. You can use one form or both, and you may complete all or only part of the forms that you use. Different forms may also be used.

Please note: If you decide to select a health-care agent that person may not be a witness to your advance directive. Also, at least one of your witnesses may not be a person who may financially benefit by reason of your death.

Form I — Living Will (Optional Form)

If I am not able to make an informed decision regarding my health care, I direct my health-care providers to follow my instructions as set forth below. (Initial those statements you wish to be included in the document and cross through those statements which do not apply.)

a. If my death from a terminal condition is imminent and even if life-sustaining procedures are used there is no reasonable expectation of my recovery —

_____ I direct that my life not be extended by life-sustaining procedures, including the administration of nutrition and hydration artificially.

_____ I direct that my life not be extended by life-sustaining procedures, except that, if I am unable to take food by mouth, I wish to receive nutrition and hydration artificially.

_____ I direct that, even in a terminal condition, I be given all available medical treatment in accordance with accepted health-care standards.

b. If I am in a persistent vegetative state, that is if I am not conscious and am not aware of my environment nor able to interact with others, and there is no reasonable expectation of my recovery within a medically appropriate period —

_____ I direct that my life not be extended by life-sustaining procedures, including the administration of nutrition and hydration artificially.

_____ I direct that my life not be extended by life-sustaining procedures, except that if I am unable to take in food by mouth, I wish to receive nutrition and hydration artificially.

_____ I direct that I be given all available medical treatment in accordance with accepted health-care standards.

c. If I am pregnant my agent shall follow these specific instructions:

_____

_____

_____

d. Upon my death, I wish to donate:

_____ Any needed organs, tissues, or eyes.

_____ Only the following organs, tissues, or eyes:

_____

_____

I authorize the use of my organs, tissues, or eyes:

_____ For transplantation

_____ For therapy

_____ For research

_____ For medical education

_____ For any purpose authorized by law.

I understand that before any vital organ, tissue, or eye may be removed for transplantation, I must be pronounced dead. After death, I direct that all support measures be continued to maintain the viability for transplantation of my organs, tissues, and eyes until organ, tissue, and eye recovery has been completed.

I understand that my estate will not be charged for any costs associated with my decision to donate my organs, tissues, or eyes or the actual disposition of my organs, tissues, or eyes.

By signing below, I indicate that I am emotionally and mentally competent to make this living will and that I understand its purpose and effect.

_____   _____
        (Date)   (Signature of Declarant)

The declarant signed or acknowledged signing this living will in my presence and based upon my personal observation the declarant appears to be a competent individual.

_____   _____
       (Witness)   (Witness)
          (Signature of Two Witnesses)

Form II — Advance Directive Part A Appointment of Health-Care Agent (Optional Form)

(Cross through if you do not want to appoint a health-care agent to make health-care decisions for you. If you do want to appoint an agent, cross through any items in the form that you do not want to apply.)

(1) I,_____, residing at _____
_____

appoint the following individual as my agent to make health-care decisions for me
_____
_____
          (Full Name, Address, and Telephone Number)

Optional: If this agent is unavailable or is unable or unwilling to act as my agent, then I appoint the following person to act in this capacity
_____
_____
          (Full Name, Address, and Telephone Number)

(2) My agent has full power and authority to make health-care decisions for me, including the power to:

a. Request, receive, and review any information, oral or written, regarding my physical or mental health, including, but not limited to, medical and hospital records, and consent to disclosure of this information;

b. Employ and discharge my health-care providers;

c. Authorize my admission to or discharge from (including transfer to another facility) any hospital, hospice, nursing home, adult home, or other medical care facility; and

d.   Consent to the provision, withholding, or withdrawal of health care, including, in appropriate circumstances, life-sustaining procedures.

(3)   The authority of my agent is subject to the following provisions and limitations:

_____

_____

_____

(4)   My agent's authority becomes operative (initial the option that applies):

_____   When my attending physician and a second physician determine that I am incapable of making an informed decision regarding my health care; or

_____   When this document is signed.

(5)   My agent is to make health-care decisions for me based on the health-care instructions I give in this document and on my wishes as otherwise known to my agent. If my wishes are unknown or unclear, my agent is to make health-care decisions for me in accordance with my best interest, to be determined by my agent after considering the benefits, burdens, and risks that might result from a given treatment or course of treatment, or from the withholding or withdrawal of a treatment or course of treatment.

(6)   My agent shall not be liable for the costs of care based solely on this authorization.

By signing below, I indicate that I am emotionally and mentally competent to make this appointment of a health-care agent and that I understand its purpose and effect.

_____   _____
(Date)   (Signature of Declarant)

The declarant signed or acknowledged signing this appointment of a health-care agent in my presence and based upon my personal observation appears to be a competent individual.

_____   _____
(Witness)   (Witness)
(Signatures of Two Witnesses)

Part B — Advance Medical Directive Health-Care Instructions (Optional Form)

(Cross through if you do not want to complete this portion of the form. If you do want to complete this portion of the form, initial those statements you want to be included in the document and cross through those statements that do not apply.)

If I am incapable of making an informed decision regarding my health care, I direct my health-care providers to follow my instructions as set forth below. (Initial all those that apply.)

(1) If my death from a terminal condition is imminent and even if life-sustaining procedures are used there is no reasonable expectation of my recovery —

_____ I direct that my life not be extended by life-sustaining procedures, including the administration of nutrition and hydration artificially.

_____ I direct that my life not be extended by life-sustaining procedures, except that if I am unable to take food by mouth, I wish to receive nutrition and hydration artificially.

(2) If I am in a persistent vegetative state, that is, if I am not conscious and am not aware of my environment or able to interact with others, and there is no reasonable expectation of my recovery —

_____ I direct that my life not be extended by life-sustaining procedures, including the administration of nutrition and hydration artificially.

_____ I direct that my life not be extended by life-sustaining procedures, except that if I am unable to take food by mouth, I wish to receive nutrition and hydration artificially.

(3) If I have an end-stage condition, that is a condition caused by injury, disease, or illness, as a result of which I have suffered severe and permanent deterioration indicated by incompetency and complete physical dependency and for which, to a reasonable degree of medical certainty, treatment of the irreversible condition would be medically ineffective —

_____ I direct that my life not be extended by life-sustaining procedures, including the administration of nutrition and hydration artificially.

_____ I direct that my life not be extended by life-sustaining procedures, except that if I am unable to take food by mouth, I wish to receive nutrition and hydration artificially.

(4) I direct that no matter what my condition, medication not be given to me to relieve pain and suffering, if it would shorten my remaining life.

(5) I direct that no matter what my condition, I be given all available medical treatment in accordance with accepted health-care standards.

(6) If I am pregnant, my decision concerning life-sustaining procedures shall be modified as follows:

_____

_____

_____

(7) Upon my death, I wish to donate:

_____ Any needed organs, tissues, or eyes.

_____ Only the following organs, tissues, or eyes:

_____

_____

I authorize the use of my organs, tissues, or eyes:

_____ For transplantation

_____ For therapy

_____ For medical education

_____ For any purpose authorized by law.

I understand that before any vital organ, tissue, or eye may be removed for transplantation, I must be pronounced dead. After death, I direct that all support measures be continued to maintain the viability for transplantation of my organs, tissues, and eyes until organ, tissue, and eye recovery has been completed.

I understand that my estate will not be charged for any costs associated with my decision to donate my organs, tissues, or eyes or the actual disposition of my organs, tissues, or eyes.

(8) I direct (in the following space, indicate any other instructions regarding receipt or nonreceipt of any health care)

_____

_____

_____

By signing below, I indicate that I am emotionally and mentally competent to make this advance directive and that I understand the purpose and effect of this document.

_____   _____
(Date)   (Signature of Declarant)

The declarant signed or acknowledged signing the foregoing advance directive in my presence and based upon personal observation appears to be a competent individual.

_____   _____
(Witness)   (Witness)

(Signature of Two Witnesses)

Virginia Advance Medical Directive

I, _____, willfully
and voluntarily make known my desire and do hereby declare:

If at any time my attending physician should determine that I have a terminal condition where the application of life-prolonging procedures would serve only to artificially
prolong the dying process, I direct that such procedures be withheld or withdrawn, and
that I be permitted to die naturally with only the administration of medication or the performance of any medical procedure deemed necessary to provide me with comfort care or
to alleviate pain

OPTION: I specifically direct that the following procedures or treatments be provided to
me: _____
_____

In the absence of my ability to give directions regarding the use of such life-prolonging
procedures, it is my intention that this advance directive shall be honored by my family
and physician as the final expression of my legal right to refuse medical or surgical treatment and accept the consequences of such refusal.

OPTION: APPOINTMENT OF AGENT (CROSS THROUGH IF YOU DO NOT WANT TO
APPOINT AN AGENT TO MAKE HEALTH-CARE DECISIONS FOR YOU.)

I hereby appoint _____(primary agent), of
_____(address and telephone number),
as my agent to make health-care decisions on my behalf as authorized in this document. If
_____(primary agent) is not reasonably
available or is unable or unwilling to act as my agent, then I appoint _____
_____
(successor agent), of _____
(address and telephone number), to serve in that capacity.

I hereby grant to my agent, named above, full power and authority to make health-care
decisions on my behalf as described below whenever I have been determined to be incapable of making an informed decision about providing, withholding, or withdrawing
medical treatment. The phrase "incapable of making an informed decision" means unable
to understand the nature, extent, and probable consequences of a proposed medical decision or unable to make a rational evaluation of the risks and benefits of a proposed medical decision as compared with the risks and benefits of alternatives to that decision, or

unable to communicate such understanding in any way. My agent's authority hereunder is effective as long as I am incapable of making an informed decision.

The determination that I am incapable of making an informed decision shall be made by my attending physician and a second physician or licensed clinical psychologist after a personal examination of me and shall be certified in writing. Such certification shall be required before treatment is withheld or withdrawn, and before, or as soon as reasonably practicable after, treatment is provided, and every 180 days thereafter while the treatment continues.

In exercising the power to make health-care decisions on my behalf, my agent shall follow my desires and preferences as stated in this document or as otherwise known to my agent. My agent shall be guided by my medical diagnosis and prognosis and any information provided by my physicians as to the intrusiveness, pain, risks, and side effects associated with treatment or nontreatment. My agent shall not authorize a course of treatment which he or she knows, or upon reasonable inquiry ought to know, is contrary to my religious beliefs or my basic values, whether expressed orally or in writing. If my agent cannot determine what treatment choice I would have made on my own behalf, then my agent shall make a choice for me based upon what he or she believes to be in my best interests.

OPTION: POWERS OF MY AGENT (CROSS THROUGH ANY LANGUAGE YOU DO NOT WANT AND ADD ANY LANGUAGE YOU DO WANT.)

The powers of my agent shall include the following:

A. To consent to or refuse or withdraw consent to any type of medical care, treatment, surgical procedure, diagnostic procedure, medication, and the use of mechanical or other procedures that affect any bodily function, including, but not limited to, artificial respiration, artificially administered nutrition and hydration, and cardiopulmonary resuscitation. This authorization specifically includes the power to consent to the administration of dosages of pain-relieving medication in excess of recommended dosages in an amount sufficient to relieve pain, even if such medication carries the risk of addiction or inadvertently hastens my death;

B. To request, receive, and review any information, verbal or written, regarding my physical or mental health, including but not limited to, medical and hospital records, and to consent to the disclosure of this information;

C. To employ and discharge my health-care providers;

D. To authorize my admission to or discharge (including transfer to another facility) from any hospital, hospice, nursing home, adult home, or other medical care facility for services other than those for treatment of mental illness requiring admission procedures provided in Article 1 (§ 37.1-63 et seq.) of Chapter 2 of Title 37.1; and

E.	To take any lawful actions that may be necessary to carry out these decisions, including the granting of releases of liability to medical providers.

Further, my agent shall not be liable for the costs of treatment pursuant to his or her authorization, based solely on that authorization.

OPTION: APPOINTMENT OF AN AGENT TO MAKE AN ANATOMICAL GIFT OR ORGAN, TISSUE OR EYE DONATION (CROSS THROUGH IF YOU DO NOT WANT TO APPOINT AN AGENT TO MAKE AN ANATOMICAL GIFT OR ANY ORGAN, TISSUE OR EYE DONATION FOR YOU.)

Upon my death, I direct that an anatomical gift of all of my body or certain organ, tissue or eye donations may be made pursuant to Article 2 (§ 32.1-289 et seq.) of Chapter 8 of Title 32.1 and in accordance with my directions, if any. I hereby appoint_____

_____
as my agent, of _____
(address and telephone number), to make any such anatomical gift or organ, tissue or eye donation following my death. I further direct that: _____

_____

_____

(declarant's directions concerning anatomical gift or organ, tissue or eye donation).

This advance directive shall not terminate in the event of my disability.

By signing below, I indicate that I am emotionally and mentally competent to make this advance directive and that I understand the purpose and effect of this document.

_____   _____
            (Date)   (Signature of Declarant)

The declarant signed the foregoing advance directive in my presence. I am not the spouse or a blood relative of the declarant.

(Witness) _____

(Witness) _____

Appendix
Further Resources:
State Bar Association Offices

The following list of state bar associations is a useful resource for more information on wills and estate planning. You can contact these offices to get a referral to a lawyer who handles estates, trusts, and taxation issues and to get copies of standard forms such as living wills.

Alabama State Bar
415 Dexter Avenue
Montgomery, AL 36104
Tel: (334) 269-1515
Toll-free: 1-800-392-5660
Web site: www.alabar.org

Alaska Bar Association
510 L Street
Suite 602
Anchorage, AK 99501
Tel: (907) 272-7469
Toll-free: 1-800-770-9999
Web site: www.alaskabar.org

Arizona State Bar
111 West Monroe Street
Suite 1800
Phoenix, AZ 85003-1742
Tel: (602) 252-4804
Web site: www.azbar.org

Arkansas Bar Association
400 West Markham
Little Rock, AR 72201
Tel: (501) 375-4606
Toll-free: 1-800-609-5668
Web site: www.arkbar.com

California State Bar
180 Howard Street
San Francisco, CA 94105-1639
Tel: (415) 538-2000
Web site: www.calbar.org

Colorado Bar Association
1900 Grant Street
9th Floor
Denver, CO 80203
Tel: (303) 860-1115
Toll-free: 1-800-332-6736
Web site: www.cobar.org

Connecticut Bar Association
30 Bank Street
New Britain, CT 06050-0350
Tel: (860) 223-4400
Web site: www.ctbar.org

Delaware State Bar Association
301 North Market Street
Wilmington, DE 19801
Tel: (302) 658-5279
Toll-free: 1-800-292-7869 (from Kent and Sussex
Counties)
Web site: www.dsba.org

District of Columbia Bar
1250 H Street N.W.
6th Floor
Washington, DC 20005-5937
Tel: (202) 737-4700
Web site: www.dcbar.org

Florida Bar
650 Apalachee Parkway
Tallahassee, FL 32399-2300
Tel: (850) 561-5839
Toll-free: (800) 342-8011 (statewide and nationwide)
Web site: www.flabar.org

Georgia State Bar
800 The Hurt Building
50 Hurt Plaza
Atlanta, GA 30303
Tel: (404) 527-8700
Toll-free: 1-800-334-6865
Web site: www.gabar.org

Hawaii State Bar Association
1132 Bishop Street
Suite 906
Honolulu, HI 96813
Tel: (808) 537-1868
Web site: www.hsba.org

Idaho State Bar
P.O. Box 895
Boise, ID 83701
Tel: (208) 334-4500
Web site: www2.state.id.us/isb

Illinois State Bar Association
Illinois Bar Center
Springfield, IL 62701-1779
Tel: (217) 525-1760
Web site: www.illinoisbar.org

Indiana State Bar Association
230 E. Ohio Street
4th Floor
Indianapolis, IN 46204-2119
Tel: (317) 639-5465
Toll-free: 1-800-266-2581
Web site: www.inbar.org

Iowa State Bar
521 E. Locust
3rd Floor
Des Moines, IA 50309
Tel: (515) 243-3179
Web site: www.iowabar.org/main.nsf

Kansas Bar Association
1200 S.W. Harrison Street
Topeka, KS 66612-1806
Tel: (785) 234-5696
Web site: www.ksbar.org

Kentucky Bar Association
514 West Main Street
Frankfort, KY 40601-1883
Tel: (502) 564-3795
Web site: www.kybar.org

Louisiana State Bar Association
601 St. Charles Avenue
New Orleans, LA 70130-3404
Tel: (504) 566-1600
Toll-free: 1-800-421-LSBA (5722)
Web site: www.lsba.org

Maine State Bar Association
124 State Street
P.O. Box 788
Augusta, ME 04332-0788
Tel: (207) 622-7523
Web site: www.mainebar.org

Maryland State Bar Association
Maryland Bar Center
520 W. Fayette Street
Baltimore, MD 21201
Tel: (410) 685-7878
Toll-free: 1-800-492-1964
Web site: www.msba.org

Massachusetts Bar Association
20 West Street
Boston, MA 02111-1218
Tel: (671) 338-0500
Web site: www.massbar.org

Michigan State Bar
306 Townsend Street
Lansing, MI 48933-2083
Tel: (517) 346-6300
Toll-free: 1-800-968-1442
Web site: www.michbar.org

Minnesota State Bar Association
600 Nicollet Mall
Suite 380
Minneapolis, MN 55402
Tel: (612) 333-1183
Toll-free: 1-800-882-MSBA
Web site: www.mnbar.org

Mississippi Bar
P.O. Box 2168
Jackson, MS 39225-2168
Tel: (601) 948-4471
Web site: www.msbar.org

Missouri Bar
P.O. Box 119
Jefferson City, MO 65102
Tel: (573) 635-4128
Web site: www.mobar.org

Montana State Bar
P.O. Box 577
Helena, MT 59624
Tel: (406) 442-7660
Web site: www.montanabar.org

Nebraska State Bar Association
635 S. 14th Street
P.O. Box 81809
Lincoln, NE 68501
Tel: (402) 475-7091
Web site: www.nebar.com

State Bar of Nevada
600 E. Charleston Boulevard
Las Vegas, NV 89104
Tel: (702) 382-2200
Toll-free: 1-800-254-2797
Web site: www.nvbar.org

or

Reno Office
1325 Airmotive Way
Suite 140
Reno, NV 89502
Tel: (775) 329-4100

New Hampshire Bar Association
112 Pleasant Street
Concord, NH 03301-2947
Tel: (603) 224-6942
Web site: www.nhbar.org

New Jersey State Bar Association
One Constitution Square
New Brunswick NJ 08901-1520
Tel: (732) 249-5000
Web site: www.njsba.com

New Mexico State Bar
P.O. Box 25883
Albuquerque, NM 87125
Tel: (505) 797-6000
Web site: www.nmbar.org

New York State Bar Association
One Elk Street
Albany, NY 12207
Tel: (518) 463-3200
Web site: www.nysba.org

North Carolina State Bar
P.O. Box 25908
Raleigh, NC 27611-5908
Tel: (919) 828-4620
Web site: www.ncbar.com

North Dakota State Bar Association
P.O. Box 2136
Bismark, ND 58502-2136
Tel: (701) 255-1404
Toll-free: 1-800-472-2685 (In State only)
Web site: www.sband.org

Ohio State Bar Association
1700 Lake Shore Drive
Columbus, OH 43204
P.O. Box 16562
Columbus, OH 43216-6562
Tel: (614) 487-2050
Toll-free: 1-800-282-6556
Web site: www.ohiobar.org

Oklahoma Bar Association
P.O. Box 53036
1901 N. Lincoln Boulevard
Oklahoma City, OK 73152-3036
Tel: (405) 416-7000
Web site: www.okbar.org

Oregon State Bar
5200 S.W. Meadows Road
Lake Oswego, OR 97035-0889
Tel: (503) 620-0222
Toll-free: 1-800-452-8260
Web site: www.osbar.org

Pennsylvania Bar Association
100 South Street
P.O. Box 186
Harrisburg, PA 17108-0186
Tel: (717) 238-6715
Web site: www.pa-bar.org

Puerto Rico Bar Association
P.O. Box 1900
San Juan, PR 00902
Tel: (809) 721-3358
Web site: www.capr.org

Rhode Island Bar Association
115 Cedar Street
Providence, RI 02903
Tel: (401) 421-5740
Web site: www.ribar.com

South Carolina Bar
950 Taylor Street
Columbia, SC 29202
Tel: (803) 799-6653
Web site: www.scbar.org

South Dakota State Bar
222 E. Capital Avenue
Pierre, SD 57501-2596
Tel: (605) 224-7554
Toll-free: 1-800-952-2333
Web site: www.sdbar.org

Tennessee Bar Association
221 4th Avenue N.
Suite 400
Nashville, TN 37219-2198
Tel: (615) 383-7421
Web site: www.tba.org

Texas State Bar
1414 Colorado
Austin, TX 78701
P.O. Box 12487
Austin, TX 78711
Tel: (512) 463-1463
Toll-free: 1-800-204-2222
Web site: www.texasbar.com

Utah State Bar
645 South 200 E.
Salt Lake City, UT 84111
Tel: (801) 531-9077
Web site: www.utahbar.org

Vermont Bar Association
P.O. Box 100
Montpelier, VT 05601-0100
Tel: (802) 223-2020
Web site: www.vtbar.org

Virginia State Bar
707 E. Main Street
Suite 1500
Richmond, VA 23219-2800
Tel: (804) 775-0500
Web site: www.vsb.org

Virgin Islands Bar Association
P.O. Box 4108, Christiansted
St. Croix, VI 00822-4108
Tel: (340) 778-7497
Web site: www.vibar.org

Washington State Bar
2101 4th Avenue
4th Floor
Seattle, WA 98121-2330
Tel: (206) 443-WSBA (9722)
Toll-free: 1-800-945-WSBA
Web site: www.wsba.org

West Virginia State Bar
2006 Kanawha Boulevard E.
Charleston, WV 25311-2204
Tel: (304) 558-2456
Web site: www.wvbar.org

Wisconsin State Bar
P.O. Box 7158
Madison, WI 53707-7158
Tel: (608) 257-3838
Web site: www.wisbar.org

Wyoming State Bar
500 Randall Avenue
Cheyenne, WY 82001
P.O. Box 109
Cheyenne, WY 82003-0109
Tel: (307) 632-9061
Web site: www.wyomingbar.org